Saturday Night Hat

Saturday Night Hat

Quick, Easy Hatmaking for the Downtown Girl
by Eugenia Kim

TECHNICAL WRITING BY JOANNE PAEK
ILLUSTRATIONS BY ALICE KIM
PHOTOGRAPHY BY JUSTIN WILLIAM LIN

POTTER
CRAFT

New York

All rights reserved.
Published in the United States by Potter Craft, an imprint of the
Crown Publishing Group, a division of Random House, Inc., New York.
www.pottercraftnews.com
www.crownpublishing.com
www.clarksonpotter.com

POTTER CRAFT and CLARKSON N. POTTER are trademarks, and POTTER
and colophon are registered trademarks of Random House, Inc.

Library of Congress Cataloging-in-Publication Data

Kim, Eugenia.
    Saturday night hat : quick, easy hatmaking for the downtown girl / Eugenia Kim ; photographs by Justin Lin
        p. cm.
    Includes index.
    ISBN-13: 978-0-307-33794-8
    ISBN-10: 0-307-33794-4
1. Hats. 2. Millinery. I. Title.

    TT655.K46 2006
    646.5'04—dc22

                                2006018364

Printed in Singapore
Design by Omnivore
Technical Writer: Joanne Paek
Illustrator: Alice Kim
Photographer: Justin William Lin
Stylist: Alex Cassidy
Hair/Makeup: Natalie DiStephano
Patternmaker: Irina Dratva
Samplemaker: Valerie Graham
Models: Ai-Li Wang, Lindsey Huizenga, Vasinthi Kumar
General Assistant: Rosemary Saponaro
Interns: Angela Gilbert, Sarah Ide, Monique Lee Smith,
 Amanda Cho, Eugenia Wong

10 9 8 7 6 5 4 3 2 1

Contents

Introduction: Madhattin' in Manhattan

One day in January 1998, a year out of college and jobless, I went shopping in downtown Manhattan. I had recently shaved my head because of a bad haircut, and was wearing a red, guinea-feathered cloche I had made in my millinery class at the Parsons School of Design. I had constructed the hat to resemble hair in some abstract way, and wore it to avoid being mistaken for the Dalai Lama.

Several storeowners immediately took notice of my unique chapeau. By the end of the day, I had appointments with three boutiques to show my collection. The problem was, I didn't have a collection. So, I decided to make two cloche styles in many different colors. The following week, my hand-feathered cloches, in vibrant hues like lavender and electric blue, were in the windows of a few stores in downtown Manhattan. By the end of the month, Barneys New York had placed its first order. Before I knew it, I was selling hats world-wide and had dozens of famous movie stars and musicians as clients. And that's how I began making hats.

Almost every fortunate thing that's ever happened to me has occurred by accident. Since I've been clumsy and accident-prone my entire life, my ability to improvise and think on the fly has helped me to turn my mishaps into some of my best creations. During my eight years creating hats, I've discovered that design, which involves a lot of spontaneous problem solving and creative freedom, is the perfect medium for my skills. If I were to spill Diet Coke on a white hat, for instance, I would probably just dip the whole hat in my soda to make it look antiqued.

I wrote this book because I have a hard time following instructions unless they are phrased in very simple steps and explained to me over and over again. I found the instructions in other millinery guides difficult to understand, so I wanted to create a how-to book on making hats that anyone could easily follow. You could call this a "hat design for dummies" type of book. I simplified many of the techniques that I use, because this book is not necessarily for those who are studying couture millinery. In fact, most of the projects can be completed in less than an hour. Essentially, they're all designed to be made right before a big night out. Some can even be made in the time it takes to tweeze one's eyebrows—think instant gratification!

The hat instructions in this book don't call for hundreds of dollars worth of millinery equipment. Actually, many of the materials can be found in your house (or stolen from your boyfriend's crib). Also, if you can't find one of the materials, I encourage you to use something similar. For instance, I once wanted to make a pink-feathered matador hat (you know, for bullfighters), but just couldn't justify the expense of a matador block that I would only use for one design. So I pinned a tennis ball on each side of my balsa block and stretched my felt over it. The next day, after it dried, I was out wearing my pink matador hat. Keep in mind that it's not necessary to follow these instructions strictly "by the book," so to speak. The beauty of millinery is that you can improvise and experiment, and there is no harm done. Sometimes, my "mistakes" become my best-selling designs.

Saturday Night Hat contains fifteen hat how-tos and fifteen trim how-tos that cover the basics of millinery. The great thing about hats is that you can mix and match crowns and brims, and hats and trims. (If you don't know the hat lingo, there's a handy glossary at the end of the book to clarify everything.) Each chapter focuses on a different hat shape, but some of the techniques presented in early chapters also apply to projects in later chapters. For instance, the engineer cap you'll learn to make in Chapter 5 uses the same crown that you'll need for the floppy sun hat in Chapter 6.

It's not necessary, however, to read the chapters in consecutive order; all the how-tos are self-contained. Treat this book like a romance novel: Skip to the juicy parts—the ones that excite you the most. I know that not everyone will want to make a pillbox hat that looks like a sushi roll. But it will still teach you how to make a basic pillbox if you're interested.

To top it all off, *Saturday Night Hat* shares cool background history and interesting facts on each hat shape, as well as personal anec-dotes that contextualize the designs. I hope these details motivate and inspire you to make great hats of your own—for Saturday night or any time.

Now, get psyched to make some amazing hats, and most impor-tantly, have a blast!

—Eugenia Kim

Chapter 1
Rebel with a Cause: The Beret

"She walked in through the out door
... She wore a raspberry beret."
—Prince

I've worn berets during some of my finest moments. They've also helped me through my most vulnerable times. A red felt beret was the saving grace that made me happy to run into an ex on an early-morning, bad-hair-day coffee run. That same beret became exactly what I needed to look stylish and feel just a bit badass when I walked into the most important meeting of my life. This hat embodies my personality: seemingly sweet at first glance, but quite complex upon closer inspection. Berets never fail to make a statement.

Berets can be schoolgirl-innocent or Charlotte Rampling-chic. They can mark you as an artist, an intellectual, or a bohemian. Picasso and Cézanne painted in them; Joni Mitchell crooned lilting-but-subversive ballads in them; be-bereted beatniks held forth in Paris cafés and San Francisco coffeehouses, their bent heads a sea of black berets.

I always feel like a tall, willowy Parisian girl when I'm wearing a beret, even though I'm a short Korean-American. This hat has come to epitomize French chic, and also seems to be the required accessory of every French cartoon character (think Pépé LePew). However, the beret originated in nineteenth-century France as a humble, utilitarian hat worn by farmers and shepherds. I love fashion staples like overalls, headscarves, and rubber rain boots; originally worn for purely practical purposes, they've now become vehicles of personal expression. I can imagine the first girl who picked up the hat her father wore to work the field and knew it would be just the right thing to go with her school dress.

Berets have also long been associated with the military (think of the Green Berets) and no-nonsense organizations such as the Girl Scouts and the Guardian Angels. A beret is my hat of choice when I have to take care of business: I've finished collections up against a tight deadline *and* executed some of my most successful breakups with a beret tilted at just the right angle over my bangs.

As much as berets are a symbol of order and authority, they also embody rebellion. Members of the French Resistance wore them during World War II, as did *rebelles* such as Bonnie Parker (of Bonnie & Clyde fame), Patty Hearst, and Monica Lewinsky. Even though I haven't robbed a bank, joined the Black Panthers, or slept with a president, the beret's association with rebels is what I relate to most.

When I was twenty-three, I started my own company after realizing that I couldn't work for anyone else. I had only two real jobs before that: working at Domino's Pizza when I was sixteen and as an editorial assistant at *Allure* magazine right after college. Both of these jobs ended suddenly, with little room for good-byes ("Clean out your desk, and leave the building in twenty minutes"). I think it was due to my eagerness to usurp authority. (At Domino's, for instance, they thought I was good at selling pizzas; I thought I was better at restructuring and rebranding the company.) It was then that I realized that I was too strong-willed and independent to conform to corporate culture, in which kowtowing to authority figures is de rigueur.

Generally, I'm opposed to anything that hinders the creative process. I have a somewhat lawless, irreverent approach to millinery, but I promise to be gentle with you. Are you ready for your first hat-making experience?

WEAR IT WELL: FRENCH DRESSING

Berets look great on girls with thick bangs and long hair. You know that willowy, sixties' French actress look—pale face, red lips, dark hair? I was so keen to channel this look that my hairstylist insisted that I leave my beret on during my last haircut. When wearing a beret, hair looks great either down or in a French chignon. My stylist Yoko invented a cross between a chignon and a side pony just for this hat—très chic!

A strong lip is a must for the beret. In lieu of classic red lips, I like wearing red in lip gloss form to make it a bit more modern. For a French ingénue look, nothing accessorizes your fruit-shaped chapeau better than rosy cheeks that look as though they've been freshly pinched. So, dab some pink blush with your fingertips on the apples of your cheeks, and top it off with an innocent expression of exclamation.

I like berets paired with a plaid miniskirt for that Lolita/schoolgirl look or worn à la beatnik-meets-rocker with a black, ribbed turtleneck, and long, skinny black jeans. And don't forget to smoosh your beret to the side for some added attitude.

Doin' It the Che Way:
The Classic Beret

WHAT YOU NEED:

WHAT YOU NEED:

- ❑ ¹/₂ yard (.5m) of fabric (any color, any fabric content)

  TIP: *Why not cut up the plaid skirt from your fifth-grade school uniform?*

- ❑ ¹/₂ yard (.5m) of lining (any color, any fabric content)

  TIP: *If the beret istself is a solid color, I always choose a fun, flirty fabric for the lining just to spice up the design with a little "surprise". A hat with a cute lining is like racy lingerie worn underneath a black or navy business suit.*

- ❑ Tape measure
- ❑ Compass and pencil
- ❑ 12" x 12" (30.5 x 30.5cm) minimum square of paper
- ❑ Scissors
- ❑ Straight pins
- ❑ Sewing machine
- ❑ Pressing iron
- ❑ Pressing board
- ❑ All-purpose thread (color to match fabric)

  TIP: *This pattern is based on a 22½" (57cm) head circumference.*

This beret, a favored style of the revolutionary Che Guevara, is always the first hat one learns in millinery class because it is supposed to be one of the easiest styles to make. However, I can't really follow simple "how-tos," and six sessions into my millinery class, I was still working on the classic beret while everyone else had moved on to more difficult chapeaux. These über-simple directions make it easy to master this basic hat style in a few hours.

HOW TO MAKE THE CLASSIC BERET:

1. With the tape measure, calculate the head circumference the hat must accommodate. Start with one end of the tape at the center of the forehead, and bring the tape around the back of the head to meet the first end of the tape at the center of the forehead.

CREATING THE BERET TEMPLATE . . .

2. With the compass and pencil, draw a 5¾" (14.6cm)-radius circle (11½" [29cm] diameter) on the piece of paper. With the scissors, cut out the circle along your pencil line. *(This measurement is recommended, no matter what your head size.)*

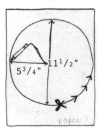

3. With the compass and pencil, draw a 3⅛" (8cm)-radius hole (6¼" [16cm] diameter) at the center of the circle. Cut it out. Your template should now look like a doughnut!

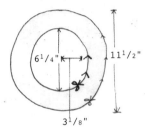

If your head circumference is smaller or larger than 22½" (57cm), follow this formula to find the diameter of the inner circle of the template:

Head circumference divided by 3.14 (pi), minus 1" (2.5cm). Then round up to the nearest ¼" (.6cm).

UTTING OUT THE PIECES
OF FABRIC . . .

4. With the scissors, cut out a
    23½"-x-3" (60 x 7.6cm) strip
    of self fabric—this will be the
    band of your beret. Set this strip
    aside.

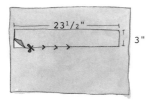

    *(If you have a smaller or larger
    head measurement than 22½"
    [57cm], add or subtract 1"
    [2.5cm] to your head measure-
    ment (for seam allowance) but
    keep the width at 3" [7.6cm].)*

5. Pin the paper template to the
    right side of the self fabric.
    Trace and cut around the out-
    side edge of the template. Set
    this piece aside. *(Leave this first
    piece as a solid circle of fabric.)*

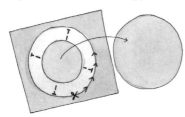

6. Pin the paper template to the
    remaining self fabric. Trace and
    cut around the outside edge of
    the template. Then trace and
    cut out the hole along the inside
    edge. *(This second piece of fabric
    should look like your template.)*

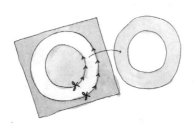

MAKING THE CLASSIC
BERET . . .

7. Pin the two pieces of self fabric
    together, right side to right side.
    Sew along the outside edges of
    the two circles with a ½" (1.3cm)
    seam allowance.

    TIP : *For a cleaner curve line, clip 3/8"
    (1cm)-long slits along the seam
    allowance at 1/4" (.6cm) intervals.*

8. Turn the shell right side out and
    press seam flat with pressing
    iron and steam.

9. Take the 23½"-x-3" (60 x 7.6cm)
    strip of self fabric that you set
    aside earlier and pin the edges of
    the shorter ends together, leav-
    ing a ½" (1.3cm) seam allowance
    on each side. Sew the ring closed.

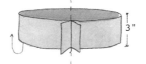

10. Fold the strip in half lengthwise,
    making it 1½" (3.8cm) wide.
    Hide seam allowance to inside.

11. If you are lining the beret,
    repeat steps 5 and 6 with the
    lining fabric. Sew the circles of
    lining fabric together, as you did
    the shell.

12. Place the lining shell inside the
    self shell, so that the seam
    allowance is hidden from the
    outside.

13. Pin the raw edge of the head-
    size band to the inside
    ("doughnut hole") circle edge
    and sew together with a
    ½" (1.3cm) seam allowance.

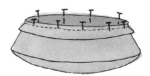

14. Turn down the headband.
    With a pressing iron, press with
    steam along the seam line
    to flatten.

Now you're ready for action!

A BERET NEW WORLD: VARIATIONS ON A CLASSIC

Think of the classic beret as a blank canvas. Because of its simple, circular shape, it's the perfect platform for your wildest embellishment fantasies. Try one of these ideas, or make up one of your own!

 Miss Pacman . . . Sew a pie-shaped piece of black leather onto a yellow leather beret. Add a black button eye and a hot pink bow and you're ready for level two!

 Flava Flav . . . Sew embroidered Roman numeral patches (I–XII) all around a cream canvas beret. Add two watch hands, and you're chasing Brigitte Nielson!

 Chocolate Chip . . . Glue or hand-sew chocolate-colored crystals onto a camel wool beret and you're one hot cookie!

 Wild Cat . . . Sew two triangle-shaped "ears" onto a leopard-print beret. Add three small, black buttons for eyes and nose and thin black leather strips for whiskers. Welcome to the jungle!

A FEW OF MY FAVORITE FRENCH THINGS

- **Onward Kashiyama** on the St. Germain-des-Près has the best accessories!
- **Mokuba**—for luxe Japanese ribbons
- **Gauloises Blondes** cigarettes—deliciously bitter!
- **Monoprix**—where I go to stock up on cheap, colorful tights
- **Darphin** skin-care products
- **Hotel Crillon**—order the decadent spread of french fries from room service when you have the munchies
- **Sonia by Sonia Rykiel**—anything and everything in the store
- **Le Bon Marché** supermarket has great cheese and chocolate
- **Muji**—for chic, minimalist office supplies
- **Anaïs Nin**—read her to get into the mood for *l'amour*
- **Belle de Jour**—Catherine Deneuve all the way!
- **Louis Vuitton** for hatboxes and cigarette cases
- **L'Escargot**—where they only serve escargots—yummy!

Playful, campy, and cute, the nub is like the stem of a cherry, the exclamation point to any beret. I came up with the idea for the nub during my mod sixties' Rudy Gernreich-worshiping phase: I could totally picture Peggy Moffit wearing my be-nubbed beret and popping out of an oversized gift box with a look of extreme surprise on her face.

HOW TO MAKE THE NUB FOR THE BERET:

1. With the scissors, cut a 4"-x-3½" (10 x 9cm) rectangle of self fabric and fold it in half lengthwise to a height of 1¾" (4.5cm). With the pressing iron, press with steam along the fold line to flatten.

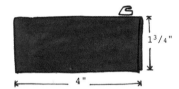

2. Fold back 1" (2.5cm) of the right end and press with iron and steam along the fold line to flatten.

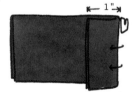

3. Roll up the rectangular piece of fabric horizontally (like a yoga mat). Roll up as tightly as possible for structure.

4. With the sewing needle, hand-tack the rolled-up fabric closed along the vertical overlap seam.

5. With the scissors, snip a small hole at the top center of the beret.

6. Insert the nub into the hole so that 1¼" (3.2cm) of it is visible and ½" (1.3cm) of it remains inside the beret. Hand-tack the nub tightly to the shell so that the nub stands upright. *(There is nothing more disappointing than a limp nub, especially since there's no Viagra-like cure for this problem.)*

Now you're done—hip, hip beret!

Get Up, Stand Up: The Nub for the Beret

Honey, I Shrunk the Beret: The Miniberet

WHAT YOU NEED:

- ❏ 5"-x-10" (13 x 25cm) minimum piece of fabric (any color, any fabric content)
- ❏ 4"-x-4" (10 x 10cm) square piece of foam or polyfill stuffing (1" [2.5cm]-thickness)
- ❏ Compass
- ❏ Fabric pencil
- ❏ Scissors
- ❏ Straight pins
- ❏ Sewing machine
- ❏ Pressing iron
- ❏ Pressing board
- ❏ Sewing needle
- ❏ Regular weight thread (color to match fabric)
- ❏ One 2" (5cm)-long, ready-made, spring-clasp barrette

Almost everything is cuter when miniaturized. You can make any hat mini by shrinking down the pattern on a copy machine, but my favorite is the miniberet. This design was huge in Japan, land of all things Lilliputian! You can make one for yourself as a hair accessory, or make a matching beret for your pint-sized pet. I made coordinating hot pink berets for me and my toy poodle, Cottonball, and we were quite a hit on the dog-walking circuit in Central Park!

HOW TO MAKE
THE MINIBERET:

1. With the compass and the fabric pencil, draw two 2" (5cm)-radius circles (4" [10cm] diameter) on the piece of fabric. With the scissors, cut them out.

2" radius   4" diameter

2. Pin the two circles together, right side to right side. Sew along the outside edges of the two circles with a ¼" (.6cm) seam allowance. Leave a 1" (2.5cm) space unsewn.

1"

3. With the scissors, snip ¼" (.6cm)-long slits, spaced ¼" (.6cm) apart, along the outside edge of the circles. Be careful not to cut past the seam.

¼" spacing

4. Turn the shell right side out. With the pressing iron, press with steam along the seam line to flatten. This will help to bring out the perfect curve of your seam.

5. With the compass and fabric pencil, trace and cut out a 3½" (9cm)-diameter circle of foam.

3½"

6. Stuff the foam circle into the fabric beret shell. With needle, hand-tack the 1" (2.5cm) space closed.

GUNS AND POSES

The beret has traditionally been associated with the military and the armed forces. In response, gun-toting rebels took over the symbol. Now, you can channel the most infamous of insurgents into your own killer creation with a few simple trim ideas . . . and a gun as an accessory.

Desperado	Beret	Accessory
Che Guevara	Black felt with a red star	M2 rifle
Patty Hearst	Black wool	AK47 and a pedigree
Bonnie Parker	Camel cashmere	Submachine gun
Saddam Hussein	Red sateen with a gold insignia	Smoking gun

TIP: *Instead of buying an actual gun, you can replicate this fierce look with a mini toy gun as a trim on your beret!*

MAKING THE MININUB . . .

7. With the scissors, cut a 2"-x-1" (2 x 2.5cm) strip of leftover Miniberet fabric. Fold down ¼" (.6cm) of the top edge along the entire length of the rectangle. Then fold the right edge into the center ¼" (.6cm). With the pressing iron, press with steam along the fold lines to flatten.

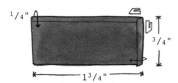

8. Roll up the rectangular piece of fabric vertically (like a yoga mat).

9. With the sewing needle, hand-tack the rolled-up fabric closed along the vertical overlap seam.

10. With the scissors, snip a small hole at the top of the beret. Inset the mininub into the hole so that ½" (1.2cm) of it is visible and ¼" (.6cm) remains inside the Miniberet. Hand-tack down the mininub from the inside of the Miniberet.

FINISHING THE MINIBERET . . .

11. Hand-tack the finished Miniberet to the holes at each end of the barrette.

12. Clip the Miniberet into your hair, or onto your pooch's fur.

Now you and your pet are totally set!

Traveling on a
Drawstring Budget:
The Drawstring Beret

One afternoon, while nursing a tequila hangover in Mexico, I came upon the idea for the drawstring beret. I was lying in my poolside cabana, dreaming of ways to remedy my post-party misery, and craving one of those old-school ice bags that Lucille Ball wore for migraines. Coupled with the drawstring pants of the senior citizens playing shuffleboard poolside next to me, the design of the drawstring beret was born!

HOW TO MAKE THE DRAWSTRING BERET:

1. With the scissors, cut out a 28"-x-9¾" (71 x 25cm) rectangle of fabric (this will be the body). Then, cut out a 23½"-x-3" (60 x 7.6cm) strip of fabric (this will be the headband).

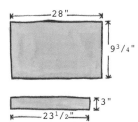

This pattern is for a 22½" (57cm) head size. If your head circumference is larger or smaller than 22½" (57cm), add or subtract the difference from the length of both rectangular pieces.

2. Fold the larger fabric piece in half lengthwise. Sew the shorter ends together with a ½" (1.3cm) seam allowance, stopping 1¼" (3.2cm) from the top edge. Leave a ¼" (.6cm) space unsewn (for the drawstring opening) and then sew the top edge.

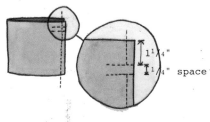

SETTING THE BODY PLEATS . . .

3. Flip so that the ¼" (.6cm) space is at the bottom. Set a ½" (1.3cm) pleat at the left corner so that the total pleat depth is 1" (2.5cm). Secure it in place with a straight pin.

pleat #1

TIP: *An easy way to keep pleats consistent is to use a straight ruler. Place your ruler tip at the pleat placement, then fold back the fabric over the ruler. Set the ruler ½" (1.3cm) below the top edge of the fabric to make room for the straight pin.*

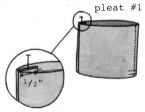

4. Rearrange the fabric "cylinder" so that the seam is vertical at the center front. Fold the second pleat (½" [1.3cm] fold, 1" [2.5cm] total depth) 3" (7.6cm) to right of seam. Secure it in place with a straight pin. Pin and secure the third pleat 3" (7.6cm) to the left of seam. (*The two pleats should be a mirror image of each other.*)

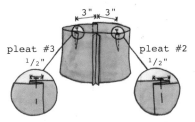

5. Center and pin the fourth pleat between pleat #2 and pleat #1.

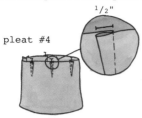

pleat #4

6. Center and pin the fifth (and final) pleat between pleat #3 and pleat #1.

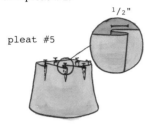

pleat #5

FINISHING THE HEAD-SIZE BAND . . .

7. Fold the 23½"-x-3" (60 x 7.6cm) strip of fabric you cut earlier in half lengthwise and pin the short ends together. Sew closed with a ½" (2.5cm) seam allowance.

8. Fold the strip in half lengthwise, making it 1½" (3.8cm) wide. Secure the raw edges at the bottom.

1½"

9. Turn the body "cylinder" upside down so that the pinned pleats are set to the bottom. Turn the body "cylinder" right side out so the seam allowance is now set to the inside.

10. Layer the folded headband over the body, lining up the bottom edges of the headband with the pleated edge of the body, and pin the two pieces in place. Line up the vertical seam lines of the body and the headband. Sew all three raw edges together with a ½" (1.3cm) seam allowance.

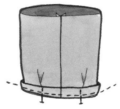

11. Turn down the headband, setting the seam allowance up. With the pressing iron, press along this seam line to flatten.

MAKING THE DRAWSTRING TUNNEL . . .

12. To make the drawstring tunnel, fold 1" (2.5cm) of the top edge into the inside of the beret. Sew down with a stitch line ¾" (2cm) from the folded edge. (The ¼" [.6cm] gap in the seam will line up and become the drawstring "hole.")

1"

¾"

13. Pin a safety pin at the end of the ribbon (the drawstring) and feed it through the tunnel.

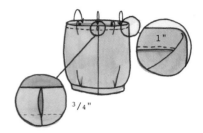

14. Pull the drawstring to your desired head size and tie a bow or double knot to secure.

Now, you're ready to rock and roll!

. . . .

BERET FOR HOLLYWOOD

Norma Shearer in *Lady of the Night* (1925)

Marlene Dietrich in *The Blue Angel* (1930)

Audrey Hepburn in *Funny Face* (1957)

Faye Dunaway in *Bonnie & Clyde* (1967)

Ali McGraw in *Love Story* (1970)

Madonna in *Evita* (1996)

THE INFINITE BERET

A drawstring, normally the staple of unflattering hospital wear and maternity garb, is amazingly glamorous and versatile as a beret!

1. Open the drawstring just a little bit to allow for a ponytail.

2. Loosen it a bit more and pull it back for a snood.

3. Keep it loose, then ruche it for a preppy headband.

4. Pull it over your head, and it becomes a chic turtleneck dickey.

5–6. Get creative! For instance, last December my assistant Rose was in a car accident, and for her, wearing a hideous and unfashionable neck brace was more painful than her actual injuries. For Christmas I thought of yet another way to utilize the Drawstring Beret—I made it in her favorite color cashmere—red—as a neck brace cover! Witness Rose's almost butterly-like metamorphosis!

I Want Candy!:
The Candy Trim

- ❏ 2¹/₂"-x-3" (6.4 x 7.6cm) rectangle of striped cotton jersey fabric

TIP: *On a budget? Use old baby clothes or a sock that has lost its mate.*

- ❏ 2¹/₂"-x-3¹/₂" (6.4 x 9cm) rectangle of tulle or mesh

- ❏ One 1¹/₄" (3.2cm)-diameter, dome-shaped button

TIP: *It is important to find a button that has a flat back, as this will allow the "candy" to securely lie flat when sewn down.*

- ❏ Scissors
- ❏ Pinking shears
- ❏ Sewing needle
- ❏ Heavyweight thread (color to match fabric)
- ❏ Assortment of small beads, sequins, or crystals
- ❏ Fabric glue (clear Magnatac 809 or white Sobo glue)

TIP: *Let the glue dry for a few minutes after using.*

Candy is so irresistibly cute and indulgent, à la Nermal from "Garfield." After "OD-ing" on bows one season, I saw this candy trim as a fresh antidote to my bow-beaten blues. And don't worry, you carb fearing freaks. This sweet treat is guilt-free!

HOW TO MAKE THE CANDY TRIM:

1. Cut a 2¹/₂"-x-3" (6.4 x 7.6cm) rectangle of fabric using the pinking shears to cut the shorter ends and scissors to cut the longer sides.

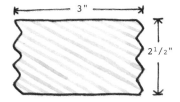

2. Cut a 2¹/₂"-x-3¹/₂" (6.4 x 9cm) rectangle of tulle, using the pinking shears to cut the shorter ends and scissors to cut the longer sides.

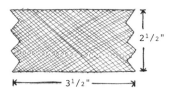

3. Place the jersey fabric rectangle back side up onto the center of the tulle rectangle.

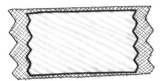

4. Place the button dome side down and flat side up onto the center of the tulle fabric "wrapper."

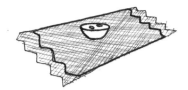

5. Hand-tack the long sides of the rectangle together tightly over the flat side of the button.

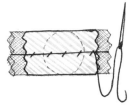

6. Twist each pinked edge of the "wrapper," pulling the fabric tight. Then hand-tack each twist to hold.

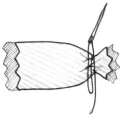

7. Hand-tack beads or glue sequins or crystals to trim the "candy" as you like. If you glue them, let the glue dry for a few minutes.

8. Hand-tack the "candy" to the hat of your choice.

Keep on makin' 'em—you can never have too much candy!

Chapter 2
Cloche Encounters

Cloches are clean and simple and easy to wear (they were worn in the twenties for tennis and golf), and at the same time, ladylike and feminine in a modern way. Due to a bad haircut, I embraced the cloche as a way of dealing with the fast pace of New York City while still looking like a girl: I can cut a path through New York's congested sidewalks without getting snagged along the way, as I would with a big brim.

The cloche was created in the early 1900s by Parisian milliner Caroline Reboux, who molded hood-like pieces of felt right onto her clients' heads for perfect custom fits. But it was Coco Chanel who put the cloche on the fashion map in the 1920s. The modern shape perfectly complemented her menswear-inspired lines.

Finally free from the shackles of college and the corporate world, and with a predilection for going out and doing all the insane things you do in your twenties, I immediately identified with the independent-minded, fun-loving flappers of the Jazz Age. The 1920s were the original girl-power decade, and my absolute favorite era. After women won the right to vote in 1920, it was *so* time to party. All the constraining corsets and bustles of Victorian times were tossed aside in favor of drop-waisted, knee-baring dresses. Up until then, the hats that women wore were wide-brimmed, veiled architectural feats, but just like the clothing, hats began to get smaller and more fitted, creating a more dance-friendly, aerodynamic line. The 1920s were the first decade when women's clothes were built for comfort and ease. The cloche made it possible (even fashionable) for flappers to roll out of bed and still look cute. With the growing popularity of the automobile, the deeper crown of the cloche allowed a woman to keep the hat elegantly perched in place while driving fast in an open car.

The cloche, which literally means "bell" in French, seemed to ring in the essence of the era——reckless freedom with the mantra of "Live for today." Girls bobbed their hair, stayed up all night, and drank gin from flasks that they tucked into the bands of their stockings. Zelda Fitzgerald, wife of F. Scott and cloche-carrying member of New York nightlife in the Jazz Age, was the first incarnation of the flapper and the model upon which all of Fitzgerald's female heroines were based. Her evening escapades, together with F. Scott, were so wild that the newspaper magnate William Randolph Hearst assigned one writer on his staff just to cover their goings-on. Meanwhile, Dorothy Parker, the sharp-witted poet who wrote for *The New Yorker* and *Vanity Fair,* managed to be both demure and scandalous in her cloche as she sat at the infamous Algonquin roundtable, drinking martinis in the middle of the day while tossing acerbic wisecracks out of the side of her mouth. She had extramarital affairs, drank heavily, and attempted suicide three times, but always maintained the high quality of her verse. While peering out from under her cloche, Anaïs Nin wrote her shocking and subversive journals. Cloche-toting women like Zelda, Dorothy, and Anaïs were intellectual and fashion pioneers in a turbulent, role-changing decade, and continue to be inspirations to girls like you and me.

WEAR IT WELL: BELL DU JOUR

Cloches look best on girls with short or bobbed hair. An asymmetrical bob makes the look more modern when paired with a cloche. Long hair can be pulled back into a low chignon or ponytail to maintain the clean line of the hat and the neckline. For more of an evening look, wear your tresses down but off to the side.

Since a cloche sits low over the forehead with eyes half-hidden, there is a fine line between looking *mysterioso* and being able to see. The cloche should be worn pulled down just enough to enable you to cross the street safely. (If you need to improve your vision in a hurry, just fold the brim up.) Since wearing a cloche brings attention to your eyes, play them up: I like to smudge my eyes with black kohl for a smutty, up-all-night look. For something more exotic, try a sharp cat's-eye wing with liquid liner in a shocking shade such as peacock green. Or skip the eye makeup entirely and do a strong red lip instead. To channel some of that dark side, go Goth with a deep burgundy lipstick.

A cloche works best on girls with square or heart-shaped faces. If you have a round face, find a cloche that has a higher crown; otherwise the bell shape may make a round face look chubby. In terms of clothing, I really dig the way a cloche looks with a long wool coat over a pair of trousers. Add a silk or chiffon ruffled blouse to set off the cloche's feminine vibe. I also love to pair this hat with a slightly torn flapper dress over a pair of jeans and with tons of long, clashing necklaces. The Haircut Hat is great with an East Village punk rock look; try a tight, sleeveless T-shirt with jeans or go classic with a vintage cocktail dress.

Cloche Call:
The Classic Cloche

WHAT YOU NEED:

- ❑ ¹/₂ yard (.5m) of fabric (any color, any fabric content)

TIP: *You can create a "patchwork" look by varying the fabrics for each panel—either pick six different fabrics or alternate solids and prints.*

TIP: *Use a waterproof vinyl fabric to make this style into a rain hat.*

- ❑ ¹/₂ yard (.5m) of lining (any color, any fabric content)
- ❑ Scissors
- ❑ Straight pins
- ❑ Sewing machine
- ❑ Regular weight thread (color to match fabric)
- ❑ Sewing needle
- ❑ Pressing iron
- ❑ Pressing board

My mother bought me a Singer sewing machine that stayed relatively unused for years—until the day David LaChapelle, the world-famous fashion photographer and my personal favorite shutterbug, commissioned my cloches in primary-colored, rainproof vinyls for a photo shoot only two days away. I worked through two sleepless nights until I got the right shape, and learned to sew in the process. This pattern—a six-panel, tailored cloche like the one Coco Chanel wore—is the fruit of that labor. And the best part about this hat is that it's reversible!

HOW TO MAKE THE CLASSIC CLOCHE:

1. See page 138 for the "Cloche" triangular pattern. Photocopy it and with the scissors, cut it out to use as your template.

2. Lay the template on the self fabric and cut out six pieces. Repeat with the lining fabric.

3. Pin two pieces of self fabric together, right side to right side. Sew them together along one side edge with a ¹/₂" (1.3cm) seam allowance.

4. Pin a third piece of self fabric to the two sewn pieces and sew together.

5. Repeat steps 3 and 4 with the remaining three pieces.

6. Pin together the two half-crown pieces, securing a pin at the top point and sew closed in a continuous stitch with ¹/₂" (1.3cm) seam allowance.

TIP: *For a cleaner curve line at all seams, snip ³/₈" (1cm) - long slits along the seam allowances at ¹/₄" (.6cm) intervals. With the pressing iron, press open the seams.*

TIP: *For a more finished look, sew topstitch to both sides of seams.*

7. Repeat steps 3 to 6 with the lining fabric. Then turn the finished lining right side out (so that you cannot see the seam allowance from the outside).

8. Place the self fabric piece seam allowance to outside over the lining seam allowance to inside.

9. Pin the shell and lining together. Sew along the bottom edge with a ½" (1.3cm) seam allowance, leaving a 2" (5cm) space unsewn, centered at one panel.

10. Turn the cloche inside out through the 2" (5cm) space. Then hand-tack the 2" (5cm) space closed.

11. With the pressing iron, lightly press with steam along the seam line for a flatter finish, especially at the brim edge.

Now, just bob your hair, throw on this cloche, and you're ready for a night out!

TRIMMING DOWN: EASY TRIM IDEAS FOR THE CLASSIC CLOCHE

After making the Classic Cloche, you may want to spice it up with a trim or two:

Feather in My Cap

Add a feather or two (or even a fan of feathers) onto your cloche. Feathers can be easily found in your local craft emporium; or for vintage feathers, scour your local flea market.

The Kids Are Alright

Raid the children's sections of stores. Trim your cloche with toy cars or tie a little boy's necktie around it.

Charmed, I'm Sure

Take an old gold chain, a pearl necklace, or add charms to your liking, and drape the chain around your cloche.

Word Up

Take a plain ribbon and write your favorite saying, song lyric, or quote on it, and sew the ribbon onto your hat (words are not just for T-shirts anymore).

HITS CLOCHE TO HOME: OTHER CLOCHE TRIMS

Hole-y Hat!

For a more decorative look, use metal grommets to reinforce the holes. Grommets can be found in any fabric store, with kits to apply them. They come as small as ¼" (.6cm) and as large as 1" (2.5cm), so play around with the proportions!

Asym Brim

For added attitude, cut the brim edge asymmetrically, so the left side is lower than the right side.

Shoe In

For a more intricate ribbon technique, punch two rows of holes (one above the other) all around the hat and thread the ribbon through the holes like a shoelace.

Of Corset!

For a corseted look, make two matching rows of holes up the back of the hood and stitch it up with ribbon.

It's a Pinch

Punch just a couple of holes at the nape of the neck and loop a bow through them to form a pinched shape.

Bohemian Rhapsody

You can also use woven straw for this cloche. Unlike felt, straw frays when cut—fray more for a boho chic look à la Jane Birkin on holiday.

Silk Stalkings	*Brooch the Subject*	*Surreal Deal*	*Flower Power*

Take an old silk scarf and wrap it around the cloche. Go through your mother's or grandmother's scarf drawer —both probably have tons of them!

Find a one-of-a-kind vintage brooch covered in rhinestones and pin it onto a plain cloche to add some bling. Go to flea markets or your local vintage store and comb through them for these unique treasures.

Make use of found objects or souvenirs— a seashell, a champagne cork, or an old key— as quirky additions to your cloche.

Pick a fresh flower or one from a bunch that your boyfriend gave you and pin it onto your cloche for the night. Lilies are most unusual and elegant, but experiment with your favorites.

Girls in the Hood:
The Felt Hood
Free-Form Cloche

WHAT YOU NEED:

- ❑ 1 felt hood

  TIP: *Hoods are preformed, cone-shaped pieces of felt that can be bought at any millinery supplier; many online suppliers will ship directly to you.*

- ❑ Tape measure
- ❑ Fabric pencil
- ❑ Metal hole puncher (a regular hand-held hole puncher from an office supply store)
- ❑ Scissors
- ❑ 1 yard (1m) of 1" (2.5cm)-wide ribbon

  TIP: *To change the mood of the piece, use velvet or satin ribbon for a dressy look, striped grosgrain ribbon for a fun look, or old shoelaces for something unexpected.*

New York is a city of immediate gratification and endless possibilities. Even by city standards, I am a particularly impatient person who prefers getting things right away (like, yesterday!) and just right. What I love about millinery is that you can make a hat by yourself, exactly the way you want it, in the time it takes to have a pizza delivered. Especially easy to make, this felt free-form cloche allows plenty of room for your own individual taste.

HOW TO MAKE THE FELT HOOD FREE-FORM CLOCHE:

1. With the tape measure, measure 7" (18cm) from the center top of the crown and mark a dot on the hood with the fabric pencil.

2. Mark dots along the head circumference every 2" (5cm). Mark another line of dots 2½" (6.4cm) below the top set (this will be your cut line for the edge of the brim).

3. With the scissors, cut along the bottom set of dots for the new brim edge.

4. With the hole puncher, punch holes at each dot.

5. Weave the ribbon in and out through the holes.

6. Place the hood on your head and cinch the ribbon to fit your head. Make a knot in the ribbon to secure this measurement. Double the knot or tie a bow.

   See—it's a cinch!

WHAT YOU NEED:

- ❑ 1 vintage felt cloche (or take the ribbon out of the Felt Hood Free-Form Cloche you made on page 38)

  TIP: *The material of the base hat should be something that has texture, such as felt or straw (but not leather), so that the glue will adhere to it.*

- ❑ 24 hackle feather pads

  TIP: *In the mood for polka dots? Try guinea feathers. In the mood for tiger stripes? Try grouse feathers.*

- ❑ Fabric glue (clear Magnatac 809 or white Sobo glue)

- ❑ Spray starch

- ❑ Pressing iron

- ❑ Pressing board

Inspired by Matisse's fishbowl paintings, I once covered a hat with aqua-colored feathers, accented by little red feathers placed to look like fish. I wore it so frequently that I became known as "the girl with aqua hair." If you want a dramatic change just for the night, but don't want the permanence of coloring your hair, trim the felt hood free-form cloche you just made (sans ribbon), or just revive a tired old cloche.

HOW TO MAKE THE FULL-FEATHERED CLOCHE:

1. Remove all the old trim and glue marks from your vintage felt cloche.

TIP: *Bring the felt back to life by scrubbing it gently with a soft-hair bristle brush or high-grade sandpaper.*

2. Put fabric glue on the bottom half of the fabric backing of the feather pad and press the pad firmly onto the brim. Let the glue dry for a few minutes. *(Leave the top half unglued so that you can slide in the last pad when finishing the row).* Allow the feathers to hang below the brim edge about ½" (1.3cm).

3. Overlapping half of the previous feather pad, glue the next feather pad onto the hat. Continue gluing and overlapping until you finish the row.

4. Glue two feather pads at the top of the crown.

5. Finish the top row. Continue gluing pads around the remainder of the hat, row by row, gluing down any loose spots.

6. To set the feathers in place, spray them with spray starch (like hair spray for hair). With the pressing iron on low dry heat, smooth down any stray feathers. Press the iron in the same direction as the feathers.

Now, go ruffle up some fun!

Bird Up:
The Full-Feathered
Cloche

PROJECT

The Metamorphosis:
The Butterfly Trim

WHAT YOU NEED:

- ❑ 2 feather pads
  (choose colors that
  complement your hat)
- ❑ 2 coque feathers
  (color to match feather
  pads)
- ❑ 4"-x-¹/₄" (10 x .6cm) strip
  of black satin ribbon
- ❑ 5" (13cm) length of black
  nylon-coated wire
  (24-28 gauge, which can
  be found at your local
  hardware or craft store)
- ❑ 2 round, ¹/₈" (.4cm)-
  diameter clear crystal
  cabochons
  (crystals with flat
  backs)
- ❑ Scissors
- ❑ Fabric glue
  (clear Magnatac 809 or
  white Sobo glue)

TIP: *Let the glue dry for a few
minutes after using.*

If you don't want to go whole hog on feathers, you can make this easy feather trim. It instantly metamorphoses your plain, "caterpillar-like" cloche into an object of astounding beauty! For a more Goth look, make a moth instead!

HOW TO MAKE THE BUTTERFLY TRIM:

1. With the scissors, cut the two feather pads 1" (2.5cm) wide at the base, 3" (7.6cm) wide at the feather tips, and 1½" (3.8cm) high at the center.

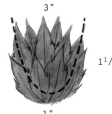

TIP: *When cutting a feather, cut it at an angle, whenever possible, to retain the feather's shape.*

2. Overlap the base of one feather pad with the other base, and glue "wings" together with the fabric glue.

3. With fabric glue, evenly spread a thin layer of glue onto the underside of the satin ribbon. Center the nylon-coated wire lengthwise at one end of the ribbon, and roll up the ribbon around the wire like a cigarette.

4. Create the "antenna" and "body" by folding the ribbon-covered wire in half and gluing it onto the center of the two feather pads, setting the overlap edge to the under side.

5. With fabric glue, glue the two small "eye" crystals in place at the base of the antennae.

6. Glue a coque feather underneath the front of each feather pad as "antenna" extensions.

7. Glue the "butterfly" to one front side of your cloche.

Now spread your wings and fly!

WHAT YOU NEED:

- ❑ One 6" (15cm) peacock or ostrich feather
- ❑ 1 feather pad (peacock or pheasant plumage feathers, or any type with a peacock-like feather pattern)
- ❑ 3 small feathers (approximately 1¹/₂" [3.8cm] long and ¹/₂" [1.3cm] wide in a color to work with the other feathers)
- ❑ 2" (5cm) length of black nylon-coated wire (24-28 gauge, which can be found at your local hardware or craft store)
- ❑ Scissors
- ❑ Fabric glue (clear Magnatac 809 or white Sobo glue)

TIP: *Let the glue dry for a few minutes after using.*

Peacocks attract their mates with their exquisite feathers. **Make this quick, easy trim, and watch the boys make "eyes" at you!**

HOW TO MAKE THE PEACOCK FEATHER TRIM:

1. With the scissors, cut the peacock feather to 6½" (16.5cm) wide at the base and 5½" (14cm) high at the center. Trim the outside edge into a fanlike shape resembling a peacock's tail.

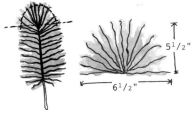

2. Cut the feather pad to 4" (10cm) wide at the base and 4" (10cm) high at the center.

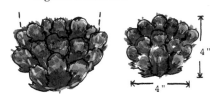

TIP: *When cutting feather pads, feathers may fall off in the process. You can always glue them back on to hide any spaces or to cover imperfections.*

3. With fabric glue, glue the feather pad over the base of the cut peacock feather. With the scissors, clip the peacock feather so that 1" (2.5cm) is visible around the feather pad.

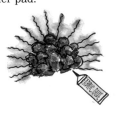

4. With the scissors, cut the stems of the three small feathers to ½" (1.3cm). Wrap black wire around both stems. Cut off the excess wire and bend the "beak" at an angle.

5. Center the "body" on top of the feather pad, setting it ½" (1.3cm) lower than the feather pad's bottom edge. Glue the "body" to the feather pad.

6. Glue the "peacock" to one front side of your cloche.

Now put on your cloche and a little "proud as a peacock" attitude!

In Full Plume: The Peacock Feather Trim

PROJECT

Hair Today,
Gone Tomorrow:
The Haircut Hat

WHAT YOU NEED:

- ☐ 24"-X-9" (61 X 23cm) sheet of thin clear plastic
  (This can be found at your local art supply store.)
- ☐ A friend
  (This project is easiest when done with a friend, preferably with a similar head size.)
- ☐ Scissors
- ☐ Clear tape
- ☐ Sharpie marker
- ☐ 1 felt hood
- ☐ Balsa wood block
  (This is a basic millinery tool that can be found at any millinery supplier--well worth the investment. When buying it, make sure to specify your exact head size.)
- ☐ Pushpins
- ☐ Fabric pencil

Angry Eugenia post-bad haircut

Forlorn Eugenia with shaved head

Happy Eugenia wearing a chic haircut hat

After a bad haircut, I shaved my head. To cover up my bald scalp, I began making these Haircut Hats that are basically felt versions of hair. They are like wigs—even chemotherapy patients buy them from me as an alternative to hairpieces. Now you can cut your "hair" any way you want.

HOW TO MAKE THE HAIRCUT HAT:

1. With the scissors, cut the clear plastic sheet to 24" (61cm) long by 9" (23cm) high.

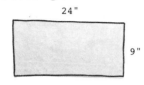

2. Tightly wrap the clear plastic sheet around your friend's head. With clear tape, tape the cylinder closed at the back (the closer to a perfect cylinder, the more accurate your "haircut template" will be).

TIP: *Do this quickly unless you have designs on suffocating your BFF.*

3. With a Sharpie marker, draw your desired "hairline" onto the clear plastic cylinder around the entire head. The clear plastic will allow you to visualize your design on your friend; make sure to keep the placement of the eyes and ears in mind.

4. Lay the clear plastic flat and cut along the new "hairline." Tape the clear plastic back into the shape of a cylinder. This will be your "haircut template."

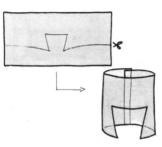

5. Soak the felt hood in hot water for ten minutes, allowing for complete saturation.

6. Wring out the hood as much as possible. It should now be pliable enough to mold over the balsa block.

7. Set the wet hood onto the balsa block and stretch it tightly from the back to the front. Gather all the excess fabric at the front bottom of the balsa block and secure it with pushpins at the bottom as you go.

8. Then stretch even more felt to the front face area of the block. You want to remove all wrinkles from the back and top of the block. Push pins into the block at the front face to secure the felt.

TIP: *Avoid any wrinkles that are left in the "hairline" area because they will be set into the felt.*

9. Let the hood dry overnight.

TIP: *For a quicker dry, leave the hooded block in the oven for twenty minutes on low heat. (Set a timer so you don't burn down the house.)*

10. When the hood is completely dry, pin the cylindrical "Haircut" template into place over the hooded block. With the fabric pencil, mark the "hairline" onto the felt.

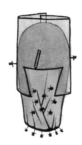

11. Undo the pushpins and remove the hood. Cut along the marked "hairline" onto the felt.

TIP: *If you stop midcut, try to keep the cut line continuous. If you don't like your line, give your hat another haircut.*

TIP: *To give your Haircut Hair "highlights," cut felt strips in a tonally lighter color. If you're making a hot pink Haircut Hat, give it light pink highlights.*

Now, put on your best "hair-ess" attitude, and party like Paris!

- -

FROM HAIR TO ETERNITY: FAMOUS HAIRCUTS TO INSPIRE YOU

When designing your Haircut Hat, think iconic:

Elvis
I've always wanted to have a pompadour like Mr. Presley's. To get the heightened benefits of the King's mane, just cut some sideburns around the ear and a curl in the middle of the forehead. Then roll a small piece of the leftover felt and hand-sew it on top of the Haircut Hat. Now just put on some blue suede shoes!

Anna Wintour
To get this editrix's look down pat, create straight-across "bangs" and cut the rest into a bob with sharp angles. You're in *Vogue*!

Catwoman
Using a leopard-print felt, cut the "Anna Wintour" but make the "bangs" cover your eyes and come down just above your nose. Then cut out almond-shaped eyeholes. You'll be feline good!

Josephine Baker
Cut a "part" on the left side of the Haircut Hat. Then, cut curlicues of felt cascading down from the left "part" to the right side to frame one side of your face. Trim with feathers, and be very scantily clad otherwise. *Très* Josephine!

- -

Chapter 3
Shaken, Not Stirred: The Cocktail

My favorite hats to wear are cocktail hats. While other hats protect from the sun or snow or even bad hair, the cocktail is the most frivolous and least necessary of chapeaux. It has no other function than to embellish (read: make you look like a rock star!). Since I have the round, flat face common to Korean girls, I find the cocktail hat to be a natural face-lift, as the eye draws upward to the mini-chapeau.

Cocktail hats can be dangerously attention-grabbing. Greta Garbo wore cocktails that created an air of mystery and added a feminine touch to her menswear-inspired looks. But you don't need to be a movie star or go to a party as an excuse to wear a cocktail; even a trip to the corner deli or supermarket becomes glamorous when you're wearing one.

Some say that the original "cocktail hats" came about during the Revolutionary War when American soldiers stole some male pheasants from the detested invading British officers, plucked the birds' tail feathers, attached them to their hats, and threw a wild party. While drinking, they toasted Betsy, a barmaid in Hall's Corners, New York: "Here's to the divine liquor which is as delicious to the palate as the cocks' tails are beautiful to the eye!" To which a French officer replied, *"Vive le cocktail!"*

With the advent of the 1930s, girls were tired of looking like boys, and ladylike became hip again. One effect of Prohibition in the 1920s was that cocktail parties became all the rage. With cocktail parties came cocktail dressing, the predecessor of modern dressing. Instead of the hassle of changing their outfits three or four times a day, women streamlined their day-to-evening look with only a cocktail hat to distinguish the two. Cocktail hats also complemented the updos that were trendy during this time.

When materials became rationed commodities in the wartime forties, hemlines were hiked and utility fashion became de rigueur. Since rations didn't extend to feathers, veiling, and artificial flowers, the cocktail hat was the one area in fashion where a girl could still go all out and be frivolous. In Nazi-occupied France, the cocktail hat became known as the "pièce de résistance" because it was a symbol of rebellion against an otherwise austere, wartime look.

Hats became less common in the postwar forties and fifties, mainly showing up in the form of small, unobtrusive cocktail hats. During the 1960s, as hair became bigger, hairstyles replaced the hat as the more elaborate mode of feminine expression, and hats took a backseat in the form of little veiled concoctions and pillboxes perched on the back of the head.

Cocktails are the most sculptural of hats: You can make them into any shape as long as they attach to your head by an elastic band or a comb. They allow you the most freedom of expression when designing, and your own sense of humor to shine. I particularly admire the cocktail creations of Elsa Schiaparelli, a super-flamboyant surrealist who hung out with Dali, Cocteau, and Stravinsky. Living and working in 1930s Paris during the city's cultural heyday, Schiaparelli married art and culture to fashion, rather than simply sticking to trends as did her fashion counterparts.

For her, as for me, the cocktail hat became the perfect platform for one's wildest surreal fantasies. She made a shoe hat, a pincushion hat, and my all-time favorite—a birdcage hat with canaries inside. I've made an ashtray crown with crystal ashes and snakeskin cigarette "butts" to top off a princess-cut dress for an East Village "aristocrat" look. Whatever you choose to create, don't take yourself too seriously, and wear it with confidence when steppin' out!

**WEAR
IT WELL:
MIX AND MATCH**

Cocktail hats are classically worn with the hair pulled back and with a little black dress. Update this look by pairing the cocktail with a T-shirt, jeans, and hair worn down and slightly messy. By doing this casual/dressy combo, you'll look like the epitome of downtown chic instead of like a bad 1940s' flashback in a cocktail dress.

I like to wear dark eye shadow and tons of black eyeliner with cocktail hats. You might try a bright color like fuschia on the lids, which is especially striking when the cocktail hat is paired with a veil. You can also create drama with blush, as the cocktail tends to emphasize cheekbones (even if you don't have them).

Position is key when wearing a cocktail hat. Jackie O. wore her pillboxes toward the back of the head. My preference for hat placement is to position it slightly askew and toward the front, on the opposite side of your part. If you want to cover up a lazy eye, make sure the veil goes over *that* eye. Whatever you do, don't wear the cocktail hat in the middle of your head—so nerdy! Remember, asymmetry equals attitude. Most importantly, cocktail elastics should be worn under your hair so they're not visible, and not under your chin—unless the look you're going for is monkey chic or band geek.

Feline Groovy: The Hello Kitty Cocktail Hat

WHAT YOU NEED FOR THE COCKTAIL FRAME:

- ❏ 8" (30.5cm) square of buckram or double buckram
- ❏ CD of last year's favorite band
- ❏ Bowl with 4³/₄" (12cm) base (or any object with a smooth, round surface, such as a basketball)

TIP: *This will determine the amount of curve your domed cocktail frame will have.*

- ❏ ¹/₄ yard (.25cm) of any white Fleece fabric (or white cashmere wool for the luxe kitty)
- ❏ ¹/₄ yard (.25cm) of red felt lining fabric
- ❏ 2 black ¹/₄" (.6cm)-diameter round plastic buttons
- ❏ 1 yellow ¹/₄" (.6cm)-diameter round plastic button
- ❏ Fabric pencil
- ❏ Straight ruler
- ❏ Scissors
- ❏ Pressing iron
- ❏ UHU glue stick

TIP: *Let the glue dry for a few minutes after using.*

- ❏ Sewing needle
- ❏ Heavyweight black thread
- ❏ Straight pins
- ❏ Sewing machine
- ❏ Regular weight white thread
- ❏ 1 elastic cording cocktail hat strap with metal tips

WHAT YOU NEED FOR THE BOW:

- ❏ 6" (15.25cm)-length minimum of ¹/₂" (1.3cm)-wide red satin ribbon
- ❏ Straight pin
- ❏ Sewing needle

At one point in her life, every girl falls in love with Hello Kitty. Hello Kitty is a passive-aggressive Asian girl who says little (she has no mouth!). The end result: a huge gain (she is world famous and loved by many!). To celebrate Kitty's thirtieth birthday, I captured her pure, graphic, yet feminine look on a small, round cocktail. Now you too can cherish Le Kitty by making this hat.

HOW TO MAKE THE HELLO KITTY COCKTAIL HAT:

TIP: *Ready-made cocktail frames in many different shapes and sizes are available at your local millinery store. I prefer to make my own.*

1. Place the CD on the buckram square. With the fabric pencil, trace a 4³/₄" (12cm)-diameter circle around the edge of the CD. With scissors, cut along the line.

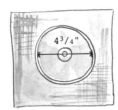

2. With your pressing iron, steam and shape the buckram circle over the bowl or another domed surface. Let the buckram cool for ten minutes until hardened.

3. Repeat step 1 with your white fabric. Trace a line ¹/₂" (1.3cm) around the circle and cut along the outside line.

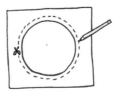

4. Repeat step 1 with your red lining fabric, but this time trace a line ¹/₄" (.6cm) to the inside of the circle.

5. With the glue stick, coat the outside of the cocktail frame.

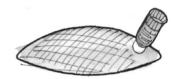

6. Center the cocktail frame on the backside of the white fabric circle and smooth out any creases.

7. With scissors, clip ¹/₂" (1.3cm)-long slits along the outside edge of the fabric. Set snips ¹/₄" (.6cm) apart from each other.

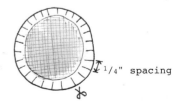

¹/₄" spacing

PARTY ON

Parties can be fun, but theme parties are much more entertaining—and are the perfect setting to show off your new hat. Get inspired by these famous soirées and party films to throw your own themed fête. Sometimes, especially when you have a great getup, it's much more enjoyable getting ready for a bash than actually going to or throwing one.

Boston Tea Party (1773)
Nowadays, Americans upset about having to pay taxes just complain, but back in colonial days, they did something about it: they dressed like Native Americans, threw tea off ships, and called it a party. Now you can party like it's 1773! Throw a bash on a boat right before Tax Day and chuck anyone not having fun overboard!

La Dolce Vita (1960)
Beautiful bombshell Anita Ekberg shines in Fellini's social commentary on the emptiness of the wealthy and beautiful set attending glamorous soirée after soirée. To reconstruct the film's setting, party like a rich Italian spoiled by the good life and set up blinking lights to create a paparazzi-laden atmosphere. Also, get inspired by Nadia's divorce party and rejoice in "misery loves company" style. Why not celebrate your failure instead of wallowing in it? Take a modern-day malfunction and use it as an excuse to party. If you lose your job, throw a pink-slip party where everyone has to wear a pink slip—even the boys.

Breakfast at Tiffany's (1961)
Everything I know about throwing a glamorous party in a small New York apartment I learned from this movie. To re-create the movie's ambience, have almost no furniture, invite too many guests, disturb your neighbors so the police come, and wear a vintage Givenchy frock.

Studio 54 (1977–1986)
Every eve was a celebration at this drug- and sex-fueled playground for celebs of the seventies. This is the infamous place where a half-naked Bianca Jagger rode in on a horse on her birthday, and where even Cher wasn't cool enough to get past the bouncer. Bring back the days of Studio 54! Put on some disco tunes, dress up as your fave seventies' star (or just one of the beautiful people), and create your own velvet rope. Be selective about who you let in, even if you invited everyone in the first place!

Animal House (1978)
This is the original frat house film, and is inspired, incidentally, by my alma mater, Dartmouth College. Throw an Animal House soirée in the classic frat boy way: with togas and high jinks aplenty.

Pretty in Pink (1986)
This movie brings me back to the heady days of the ultimate adolescent celebration known as the prom. I still cry when I see it, even though the story line is predictably John-Hughes eighties: Girl from wrong side of the tracks goes to the prom with geeky friend but in the end gets the high school heartthrob. Didn't get to go to your prom? You can now! The tackier the dress or tux the better. Remember to spike the punch bowl, and hold a vote for Prom Queen and King!

8. With the glue stick, glue ½" (1.3cm) of the inside edge of the frame and fold the fabric seam allowance down to the inside of the frame.

TIP: *The slit edges can overlap at the inside of the frame to allow for a cleaner, curved edge.*

9. With the glue stick, coat the inside center of the frame and place the red lining fabric on top. The lining edge should overlap the edge of the white shell fabric by ¼" (.6cm).

TIP: *For a more secure finish, you can hand-tack the lining to the shell along the overlap seam.*

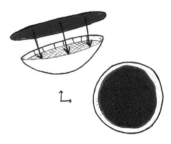

ADDING THE "EYES" AND "NOSE" . . .

10. With black thread, sew the two black plastic buttons onto the frame for Hello Kitty's "eyes" (set each button edge 1" [2.5cm] from the side edge and 2" [5cm] from the top edge).

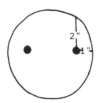

11. With white thread, sew the yellow plastic button at the center, 2" (5cm) from the bottom edge for Hello Kitty's "nose."

ADDING THE "WHISKERS" . . .

12. With a double strand of heavyweight black thread, make the "whiskers" by sewing three straight stitches ¾" (2cm) long and ¼" (.6cm) from the outside edges of her "eyes," sewing over the edge of the frame. First stitch the center "whisker" parallel to the eye, then stitch the top and bottom "whiskers" at a slight angle at the outside edge.

MAKING THE "EARS" . . .

13. With the scissors, cut out two soft triangles from the buckram scraps for Hello Kitty's "ears" 1¼" (3.2cm) wide at the base and 1¼" (3.2cm) high at the center.

14. With the fabric pencil, trace a buckram "ear" onto the leftover white fabric, adding a ¼" (.6cm) seam allowance border. Cut along the outside line for four fabric pieces total.

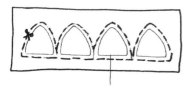

15. Pin two pieces together, right side to right side, and sew the edges closed, leaving the bottom open. Turn the piece right side out and insert the buckram. Repeat with the other "ear" and hand-tack it to the underside edge of the frame with a ½" (1.3cm) seam allowance (¾" [2cm] of the ear should be visible from the outside of the hat).

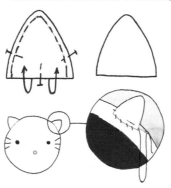

MAKING THE "BOW" . . .

16. With the scissors, cut off a 1½" (3.8cm)-long piece of ribbon and set it aside.

17. Take the remaining ribbon and fold back the ends to a finished width of 1¾" (4.5cm).

18. Wrap the separate 1½" (3.8cm) ribbon piece around the center and perpendicular to the fold-back piece.

19. Pin closed and hand-tack it closed at the back.

20. Sew the "bow" onto the frame, covering the left "ear" seam.

FINISHING THE COCKTAIL . . .

21. To set the strap hole placement, place the pillbox asymmetrically to one side of your head, depending on your hair part and the way you want to wear the hat. With the fabric pencil, mark the points on each side of the hat.

22. Take off the hat and use the pointed tips of the metal ends of the elastic strap to pierce in and out of the lining fabric ½" (1.3cm) from the edge.

23. Place the hat to a front side corner of your head and tuck the elastic strap to the back of the head, underneath your hair.

Now, you're kitten pretty!

TIP: *In the mood for something more elegant? Just cover the base with your favorite fabric (perhaps a boucle) and add some feathers or flowers to it.*

Don't Be a Pill:
The Pillbox Hat Frame

WHAT YOU NEED:

- ❏ 14" (35.5cm) square of buckram or double buckram (Double buckram is preferred because it is stiffer and can withstand a little beating up, but use whatever you can find, even cardboard.)
- ❏ Compass
- ❏ Fabric pencil
- ❏ Scissors
- ❏ UHU glue stick

TIP: *Let the glue dry for a few minutes after using.*

- ❏ 1 elastic cocktail hat strap with metal tips

Every society needs a royal. So, when Jackie Kennedy wore a Halston-designed pillbox to JFK's inauguration, the hat immediately became America's crown substitute for its first lady. Photographers loved this chapeau because Jackie's gorgeous face could be shot beautifully from every angle. Fast-forward to that fateful November day in Dallas, 1963: Jackie remained ever the lady in her pink Chanel suit and matching pink pillbox, holding her composure during even her darkest hours. This final fashion look as first lady was the one most remembered by Americans and made an icon of Jackie. You may not have as much drama in your life, but you can create your own drama with a Jackie-inspired minipillbox cocktail.

HOW TO MAKE THE PILLBOX HAT:

QUICK TIP: *Need the hat tonight? Buy a prefabricated mini-pillbox frame at your local millinery supplier or use a small empty margarine container. Then skip to page 60 trim as a Mini-cake or as page 62 as Sushi.*

1. With the compass and the fabric pencil, trace a 2" (5cm)-radius circle (4" [10cm] diameter) on the buckram sheet (this will be the top of the cylinder frame).

2. Trace a ¼" (.6cm) border around the existing 4" (10cm) circle (making a 4½" [11.5cm]-diameter circle). With the scissors, cut out the 4½" (11.5cm)-diameter circle.

3. With the scissors, snip ¼" (.6cm)-long slits along the outside edge of the circle, spacing them ¼" (.6cm) apart. Be careful to stop *just short of* the center circle line.

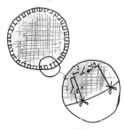

4. Bend down the ¼" (.6cm) slits, creating the "top" of the cylinder.

5. With the scissors, cut a 13½"-x-1½" (34 x 3.8cm) strip of buckram (this will be the side of the cylinder frame).

6. Shape the strip of buckram into a ring. With the glue stick, glue it around the bent slits of the top piece. When you complete the circle, glue the edges closed with a ½" (1.3cm) overlap.

½" overlap

Let Them Eat Cake:
The Minicake Pillbox

WHAT YOU NEED:

- ❑ Premade pillbox hat frame (or the frame you made on page 58)
- ❑ 12" (30.5cm) square of white stretch satin fabric

TIP: *Stretch fabrics work best for this style.*

- ❑ 12" (30.5cm) square of pink felt lining fabric
- ❑ 1 yard (1m) of 1/4" (.6cm)-wide pink satin ribbon
- ❑ Small fabric flowers
- ❑ UHU glue stick
- ❑ Scissors
- ❑ Fabric glue (clear Magnatac 809 or white Sobo glue)

TIP: *Let the glue dry for a few minutes after using.*

- ❑ Clear nail polish

Maybe if Marie Antoinette, who famously proclaimed "Let them eat cake," had been wearing this pillbox, she would have looked too cute to get beheaded. Now you can have your cake and eat it too—without gaining a pound!

HOW TO MAKE THE MINICAKE PILLBOX:

1. Use a premade pillbox frame or the one you made on page 58. With the glue stick, coat the top circle of the buckram frame. Set it on top of the back side of the lining fabric.

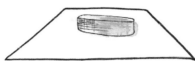

2. With the glue stick, coat the side cylinder of the buckram frame, pulling the lining fabric tightly so there are no creases or folds. (Stretch fabrics work best for this reason.)

3. With the scissors, cut off the excess fabric around the bottom edge of the frame, leaving a 1/2" (1.3cm) seam allowance.

4. Turn the covered frame upside down. With the glue stick, coat the entire inside of the frame (circle and sides).

5. Press the pink felt lining fabric into the inside the frame, securing the folds every 1 1/4" (3.2cm) along the cylinder edge.

6. With the scissors, cut the lining edge to 1/4" (.6cm) below the frame edge.

7. Fold the white stretch satin shell fabric into the inside of the frame. With the fabric glue, glue the pink felt lining edge over the shell fabric seam allowance. *(For a more secure finish, hand-tack the lining to the shell along the over-lap seam.)*

1/2" ... 1/4"

TRIMMING THE MINICAKE PILLBOX . . .

8. With the scissors, cut ribbon into two 13"(33cm)-long strips. Snip 1/2" (1.3cm) long triangles out of one end. Carefully apply clear nail polish at the cut ends to prevent fraying.

9. With the fabric glue, glue one strip of ribbon closed along the top side edge. Glue the other strip of ribbon at the bottom side edge.

10. With the fabric glue, glue fabric flowers onto the top of the Mini-cake Pillbox.

(See page 64 for strap finishing)

PROJECT

Rockin' Roll:
The Sushi Pillbox

WHAT YOU NEED:

- ❏ Premade pillbox hat frame (or the frame you made on page 58)
- ❏ 12" (30.5cm) square of white cotton stretch pique fabric
- ❏ ¼ yard (.25m) of black cotton stretch pique fabric

TIP: *If you do not have cotton pique, find any fabric with a sushi-like texture, such as honeycomb wool or snakeskin.*

- ❏ 12" (30.5cm) square of white felt lining fabric
- ❏ Five 5" (13cm)-long, thin, green feathers (see page 130)
- ❏ Thirty ⅛" (76.5 cm) round red/orange glass seed beads (color to match "tobiko," tiny red fish eggs)
- ❏ Straight ruler
- ❏ Fabric pencil
- ❏ Scissors
- ❏ UHU glue stick
- ❏ Pressing iron
- ❏ Pressing board
- ❏ Sewing machine
- ❏ Fabric glue (clear Magnatac 809 or white Sobo glue)

TIP: *Let glue dry a few minutes after using.*

Sushi is the clean, efficient culinary invention of the Japanese. You can make it into a tuna roll or a California roll. But whatever you do, you've got to "roll" with it!

HOW TO MAKE THE SUSHI PILLBOX:

1. Use a premade pillbox frame or the frame you made on page 58. Set the buckram frame on top of the back side of the white pique fabric and trace a circle around the edge of the frame. Then with the fabric pencil and ruler, trace an additional circle ½" (1.3cm) around the existing circle for seam allowance. With the scissors, cut out the fabric along the outside trace line.

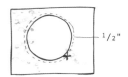

2. With the glue stick, coat the top of the buckram frame. Set the backside of the white pique fabric on top, pulling the pique fabric tightly so there are no creases or folds.

3. With the scissors, cut out a 13½"-x-2¼" (34 x 6cm) strip of black pique fabric.

4. Fold down ¼" (.6cm) of the top edge. With the pressing iron, press with steam along the fold line to flatten.

5. Sew the strip of black pique fabric into a ring with a ½" (1.3cm) seam allowance. Flip so that seam allowance is set to the inside.

6. With the glue stick, coat the sides of the buckram frame, pulling the black pique fabric ring tightly over it so there are no wrinkles or creases. Fold the ½" (1.3cm) seam allowance to the inside bottom edge of the frame.

7. With the tip of the scissors, pierce the center of the cocktail hat. Insert the green feathers, setting one at 3" (7.6cm) long, two at 4" (10cm) long, and setting two at 5" (13cm) long. Glue the "cucumber" feathers to the inside of the hat.

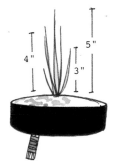

8. Turn the covered frame upside down. With the glue stick, coat the entire inside of the frame (circle and sides).

9. Press the white felt lining fabric into the inside of the frame, securing the folds every 1¼" (3.2cm) along the cylinder edge. Sandwich the feather ends in between the frame and the lining.

10. With the scissors, cut the lining edge to ¼" (.6cm) below the frame edge.

11. With the fabric glue, glue the white felt lining edge over the shell fabric seam allowance. (For a more secure finish, hand-tack lining to the shell along the overlap seam.)

12. With the fabric glue, glue each "tobiko" bead to the top "rice" surrounding the green feathers.

FINISHING THE MINICAKE PILLBOX AND SUSHI PILLBOX:

1. To secure the strap hole placement, place the cocktail hat asymmetrically on one side of your head, depending on your hair part and the way you want to wear the hat. With the fabric pencil, mark the points on each side of the hat.

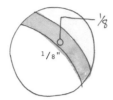

2. Take off the hat and use the pointed tips of the metal ends of elastic strap to pierce in and out of the lining fabric ½" (1.3cm) from edge.

3. Place the hat to a front side corner of your head and tuck the elastic strap to the back of the head underneath your hair.

Now, get ready to be the perfect roll model…or just have a sweet time!

PROJECT

Well Bread:
The Toast Pillbox

WHAT YOU NEED FOR THE "TOAST":

- ❑ 7" (18cm) square of buckram or double buckram
- ❑ 1 1/2"-x-1" (47 x 2.5cm) strip of buckram or double buckram
- ❑ 7" (18cm) square of white stretch cotton canvas fabric

TIP: *On a low-carb diet? Use a brown tweed fabric to make whole wheat toast, or a chunky boucle for nine-grain toast!*

TIP: *Stretch fabrics work best for this style.*

- ❑ 19"-x-3" (48 x 7.6cm) strip of light brown wool fabric
- ❑ 7" (18cm) square of white felt lining fabric
- ❑ Scissors
- ❑ Fabric pencil
- ❑ UHU glude stick
- ❑ 1 elastic cocktail hat strap with metal tips
- ❑ Fabric glue

WHAT YOU NEED FOR THE "PAT OF BUTTER":

- ❑ 1"-x-1" (2.5 x 2.5cm) square of 1/8" (.3cm)-thick cardboard
- ❑ 2"-x-2" (5 x 5cm) square of yellow silk fabric
- ❑ Fabric glue

I was inspired by the stale Wonderbread lying in my fridge, and traced a piece of it to make this hat. Soon afterward, I went to Paris and became the "toast of Paris" while wearing this little chapeau. Now, you too can become the toast of your town with this bread-shaped pillbox hat. Don't forget to add the butter! If you're lactose-intolerant, add some purple crystal beads for jelly instead! It doesn't get much butter than this.

HOW TO MAKE THE TOAST PILLBOX:

1. See page 134 for the "toast" pattern. Photocopy it and, with the scissors, cut it out to use as your template. Lay the template on the buckram and cut along the trace line. (This template includes a 1/4" (.6cm) seam allowance.)

2. With the glue stick, glue the buckram "toast" shape onto the back side of the white cotton fabric. With the scissors, cut along the buckram edge.

3. With the scissors, snip slits into the 1/4" (.6cm) seam allowance around the entire outside edge at 1/4" (.6cm) intervals. Be careful not to cut past the trace line. Fold down the slits.

4. To make the "crust," fold the top edge of the brown fabric down 1/2" (1.3cm). With the glue stick, glue both sides of the buckram strip and center horizontally onto the back side of the light brown fabric. Then press the rest of the fabric firmly onto the glued buckram.

5. With the fabric glue, coat the inside top edge of the "crust" and press it securely to the bent slits of the toast "top." With the fabric glue, glue the 1/2" (1.3cm) seam allowance to the underside of the "crust" at the bottom left corner.

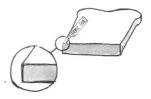

6. With the fabric glue, glue the extra 1/2" (1.3cm) of the "crust" fabric to the underside of "toast" top.

7. With the scissors, cut the paper "toast" template (from step 1) along the dotted lines, cutting off the 1/4" (.6cm) seam allowance.

8. With the fabric pencil, trace this new "toast" template onto the white felt lining fabric. With the scissors, cut out the lining fabric along the line.

9. With the glue stick, coat the underside of the "toast" top piece and firmly press the white felt lining piece into the frame. It should fit exactly.

"BUTTERING THE TOAST "...

10. With the fabric glue, coat the cardboard square and center it on the back side of the yellow silk fabric.

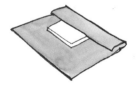

11. With the fabric glue, coat the edges of the yellow silk fabric. Fold the edges of the fabric over the cardboard square. This is the "butter." With the fabric glue, glue the "butter" to the top left corner of the "toast" (set the "butter" at an angle ¾" [2cm] from the top and ¾" [2cm] from the side; see the "toast" template for placement).

FINISHING THE TOAST PILLBOX . . .

12. To find the strap hole placement, place the "toast" asymmetrically to one side of your head, depending on your hair part and the way you want to wear the hat. With the fabric pencil, mark the points on each side of the "toast" corners.

13. Take off the hat and use the pointed tips of the metal ends of the elastic strap to pierce in and out of the lining fabric ½" (1.3 cm) from edge.

14. Place the hat to a front side corner of your head and tuck the elastic strap to the back of the head underneath your hair.

Now, get toasted!

TIP: *If you're completely anti-carb, you can create any shape now that you've got your bread and butter down pat!*

Wed 'n' Wild:
The East Village
Wedding Veil

I made this simple headband for a girl who had commissioned a veil for her summer wedding on top of an East Village rooftop that night. Ever since then I've sold this piece to a variety of women from ages twenty to forty, both uptown (with matching Manolos) and downtown (barefoot in Prospect Park). The small veil lends an air of mystery, acts as an eye shadow, gives you the Garbo look, and, as a bonus, filters out bad breath. The spray of feathers adds a bit of whimsy, and the sportiness of the headband makes it easier to dance.

WHAT YOU NEED FOR THE HEADBAND:

- ❏ 1" (2.5cm)-wide plastic headband

  TIP: *Find a vintage headband, or any drugstore brand, such as Goody, but make sure it does not have teeth on the underside.*

- ❏ 20"-x-2" (51 x 5cm) strip of paper (any type, any color)
- ❏ Fabric pencil
- ❏ Scissors
- ❏ 18"-x-1" (46 x 2.5cm) strip of foam or polyfill padding (¹/₄" [.6cm] thickness)
- ❏ 20"-x-3" (51 x 7.6cm) strip of ivory satin fabric
- ❏ 18" (46cm) length of ¹/₄" (.6cm)-wide ivory grosgrain ribbon
- ❏ Tape measure
- ❏ UHU glue stick
- ❏ Fabric glue (clear Magnatac 809 or white Sobo glue)
- ❏ Straight pins
- ❏ Sewing needle
- ❏ Heavyweight thread (color to match ivory fabric)

WHAT YOU NEED FOR THE VEIL TRIM:

- ❏ ¹/₂" yard (.5m) of ivory tulle or veiling

  TIP: *Don't be too tulle for school— tulle comes in many different varieties, from ballerina tulle with small holes to oversize-holed Chanel-style fishnetting.*

WHAT YOU NEED FOR THE FEATHER TRIM:

- ❏ Assortment of any white and ivory feathers (try coque feathers, hackle feathers, or biots)
- ❏ 3" (7.6cm) length of metal wire (24-28 gauge, which can be found at your local hardware or craft store)
- ❏ 12" (30.5cm) length of ¹/₄" (.6cm) ivory satin ribbon

HOW TO MAKE THE HEADBAND:

1. Roll the plastic headband along the strip of paper and trace the outline using the fabric pencil. With the scissors, cut out the shape along the lines (this will be your paper template).

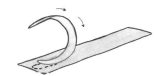

2. Set the paper template on the strip of foam or polyfill padding and cut along the paper edge. Set the foam or polyfill aside.

3. With the fabric pencil, trace the paper template onto the back side of the satin fabric, adding a ¹/₂" (1.3cm) border. With the scissors, cut along the outside line.

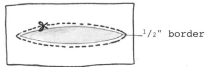

¹/₂" border

4. With the glue stick, coat the outside surface of the plastic headband and cover it with the foam cutout.

5. With the glue stick, coat the underside of the padded headband, pulling the satin fabric over it and smoothing out any creases.

6. At the ends, neatly fold the end inside, then wrap the sides over with an overlap.

7. Insert one end of the grosgrain ribbon ¹/₂" (1.3cm) deep into one finished end of the covered headband. Put a drop of fabric glue inside the fold and press firmly to secure it.

8. Then, with the fabric glue, carefully coat and secure the grosgrain ribbon over the fabric seam at center underside of headband. Press firmly into place.

9. To finish the other end, tuck the remaining grosgrain end into the fabric fold, following step 7. If needed, push the grosgrain inside with the tip of your scissors. Put a drop of fabric glue inside the fold and press firmly to secure.

TRIMMING THE HEADBAND WITH THE WEDDING VEIL . . .

10. With the scissors, cut the tulle into a 9" (23cm) wide strip. Then cut the short ends of the strip at a diagonal angle (the shorter width at the top).

11. Cinch one end along the angle and another point (9" [23cm] away) into a banana shape. Fold back the start end 1" (2.5cm) to hide the raw edge.

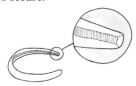

TIP: *The diagonal end will help keep the top edge of the "banana" shorter than the bottom, so that the veil is airy around the face but flush to the headband at the top edge. Keep this in mind as you gather the second cinch point, as you should adjust the tulle to keep the top edge straight but with enough fullness so that the veil does not touch your face.*

12. Using a mirror or a friend, set the covered headband on your head and artfully arrange the veil over your forehead. Anchor the veil to one side, depending on your hair part. Cinch and pin down the ends at the most flattering angle.

TIP: *The placement and size of the veil is very individual to your taste, hair part, head size, and what you want to hide and reveal. For instance, if you have a larger face, your veil should accommodate, not suffocate.*

13. After taking the headband off your head, hand-tack the pinned points to the headband. Use the same color thread as your tulle, making stitches as invisible as possible. Hand-tack the veil to the headband in two or three places along the headband.

TIP: *The top edge of the veil should be even with the headband surface. If not, pinch a tuck in the tulle before hand-tacking it to the headband to remove excess tulle length.*

14. With the scissors, cut the longer end of the tulle to your desired length, and cut the end to an angled point.

TIP: *Leave the veil longer for a traditional look; or for a more modern bridal look, cut the tulle to a shorter length.*

TRIMMING THE HEADBAND WITH FEATHERS . . .

15. Gather the feathers, experimenting with different feather types and lengths. Tightly wrap the bundle together near the feather base with wire.

16. Tie the satin ribbon in a double knot around the wire coil. Clip the ribbon ends to a diagonal point. Ribbon ends look better when asymmetrical in length; finish one end 2½" (6.4cm) and the other 4" (10cm).

17. Place the veiled headband on your head. With a straight pin, mark the most flattering feather placement. After taking off the headband, remove pin and hand-tack the back side of the ribbon knot securely to the outside of the headband. Keep the stitches invisible.

Now that you're done, you can spend your time obsessing about more important things, such as place cards and napkin sculptures.

MIX IT UP: COCKTAILS FOR YOUR COCKTAIL

What's the best accessory for your cocktail hat? A drink in your hand, of course! With these yummy recipes, you could easily be seeing double. Lucky for you, this hat won't further block your vision. Combine your concoction with a matching headpiece using these simple drink recipes and trim ideas!

WHITE RUSSIAN

Vodka, kahlua, cream, ice

Cocktail Hat Trim

Trim the edge of your white cocktail with fox fur or faux fur to look like a Russian princess.

SHIRLEY TEMPLE

Ginger ale, dash of grenadine

Cocktail Hat Trim

Tame your underaged curls with a primary -colored cocktail hat trimmed with a vintage buckle.

SIDECAR

Brandy, lemon juice, cointreau, sugar to coat

Cocktail Hat Trim

Garnish your hat with some Matchbox cars.

MINT JULEP

Mint leaves, sugar, dash of bourbon, ice

Cocktail Hat Trim

Cover your chapeau with some good, old-fashioned cotton seersucker and add some fresh leaves.

MANHATTAN COCKTAIL

Irish whiskey, vermouth, sugar to coat

Cocktail Hat Trim

Pin mismatched brooches of every kind and all those single earrings onto your cocktail hat.

LONG ISLAND ICED TEA

Vodka, gin, white rum, tequila, triple sec, lemon juice, dash of gomme syrup, cola

Cocktail Hat Trim

Top off your big hair with a leopard-print mini-chapeau garnished with thick gold chains.

KAMIKAZE

Triple sec, vodka, lime juice, garnish with lime

Cocktail Hat Trim

Get your bedazzler and create a crystal skyline on a black satin cocktail.

SINGAPORE SLING

Gin, cherry brandy, sugar syrup, fresh lime juice, dash of bitters, soda water

Cocktail Hat Trim

Chill with a cocktail hat covered with red silk shantung or an Asian-inspired silk. Trim your creation with those little colorful umbrellas from your drink.

Chapter 4
From Gangsters to Gangstas: The Fedora

There's nothing sexier than a fedora on a man . . . except a fedora on a woman. A woman in a fedora projects a strong, tough kind of sexiness. This hat is for the woman who's not afraid of embracing her masculine side. She can take care of herself as well as take care of business. With her eyes half-shaded by the tilt of her trilby, she projects a mysterious aura.

The first fedora I owned I made myself. It was a black-and-white, ocelot-print, asymmetrical number with a hot-pink band. The loud colors and graphic pattern of my hat were inspired by the zoot-suited gangsters who wore it back in the 1930s.

During Prohibition, the soft, all-purpose fedora became the hat of choice for the lawless, often unscrupulous, mavericks of society— the gangsters. Al Capone, the notorious kingpin of organized crime who practically owned Chicago, was rarely seen without his black-banded, wide-rimmed, off-white fedora. Soon, Hollywood characters, detectives, newspaper reporters, and crime-fighting comic-book heroes also picked up this tough-guy look. Later, it became a clichéd symbol of the man's man. My fave fedora caricatures include Indiana Jones, Dick Tracy, Michael Corleone, and Inspector Clouseau, the bumbling detective in *The Pink Panther*.

The fedora was also worn in films like *Casablanca* and brings to mind the old-school manners of the true gentleman. It's the kind of hat your grandfather probably wore. In those days, it was considered bad form to be seen without proper headwear. So, even if your man shoots people for a living, you know he's taking care of you, lighting your cigarette, and walking on the side nearest the street. He's looking out for you, kid!

Gangsters were rarely seen without an entire uniform: the trench coat, the three-piece suit, the cigarette, and the hat. Mobsters were men of fashion, as fashion symbolized status and money to them, and so the clothes made the man. In subsequent decades, clothes became more casual, hats became almost obsolete, or rather highly optional, for men, until the arrival of hip-hop.

Hip-hop artists and rappers reinvented the old-school fedora, and made it a requisite part of a fresh urban uniform. Artists such as Notorious B.I.G., Snoop Dogg, and Diddy helped bring the fedora back into the domain of cool. Like their 1920s' counterparts, these new wise guys are badass and sometimes get into trouble (think Biggie and Tupac). They too focus on their appearance, taking the time to coordinate an entire look, whether it's a suit, some bling, and a pimpin' hat, or the right kicks, an oversized hoodie, and a doo-rag. Now even female recording artists such as Mary J. Blige, Jennifer Lopez, and Lauryn Hill and Hollywood actresses like Nicole Kidman are wearing fedoras.

To me, wearing a fedora is a way of projecting strength and business savvy. Since I have no poker face, the fedora works well to mask my facial expressions. In general, when I need to "take care of business," I rely on the fedora to give off a "Don't mess with me" sense of authority.

TRIM SHADY

Like most good menswear accessories, the fedora is all about the details. You can completely transform a plain hat with different ribbons and feathers to suit your mood or your personality. Trim is the accessory to this ultimate accessory. In the following pages, I'll show you so many ways to trim your fedora that it may suffer from schizophrenia! Starting with a pre-fab fedora, you'll learn how to make four different types of hatbands. Then we'll go over two accent trims: feathers and fans. You can mix and match the band trims and the spot trims together in any combination that you like. The most important thing to remember is that there are endless possibilities when trimming a hat. Just keep your mind open to new ideas and the creative juices flowing at all times!

WEAR IT WELL: LOOK FEDORABLE!

I like fedoras with hair worn down since long, flowing locks offset the hat's masculinity. With hair up, you may be mistaken for a man! Soft, feminine makeup contrasts nicely with the sharp lines of this hat. I like a little lip gloss and some peach-colored blush to accentuate the cheekbones that already get a little face-lift from this hat!

Fedoras look good on everyone except women with really angular faces. With a round face, the hat will create geometry where there is none. I like to wear the fedora flipped up either in the back or on one side, to create asymmetry—*the* crucial detail for a fedora to be flattering. To make your trilby asymmetrical, gently curve one side of the brim using four fingers to massage the brim edge wire into a smooth, upward curve. (If you only use one or two fingers, the brim will look bent rather than curved.)

In terms of clothing, juxtapose the masculinity of this pimpin' shape with a delicate, floral sundress or something girly. Remember not to be too literal! Also, a fedora looks at home with a mix of other menswear-inspired pieces coupled with feminine touches. Pair it with a silk camisole and cuffed trousers, or a button-down Oxford and a short skirt.

That's So Knot Cool: The Grosgrain Trim with Cross-Knot

WHAT YOU NEED:

- ❑ Vintage fedora hat
- ❑ 1 yard (1m) of 1¼" (3.2cm)-wide grosgrain ribbon (any color)
- ❑ Scissors
- ❑ Pressing board
- ❑ Pressing iron
- ❑ Sewing needle
- ❑ Heavyweight thread (color to match grosgrain)

Grosgrain ribbon is a classic hat trim for fedoras, and the knot just gives it that couture millinery finish. The beauty is that it only takes ten minutes to make. In the time that it takes to microwave a meal, you're out the door. I'm with this band!

HOW TO MAKE THE GROSGRAIN TRIM WITH CROSS-KNOT:

1. Wrap the length of grosgrain around the outside circumference of your fedora, where the brim meets the crown (the rope line). With the scissors, cut the grosgrain length so that there is a 1" (2.5cm) overlap.

2. Place the grosgrain flat on a pressing board. With the pressing iron, press with steam, pulling the bottom edge of the ribbon into a curve. When finished, you should have a soft, even curve along the entire length of the grosgrain.

3. With the sewing needle, hand-tack one end of the grosgrain ribbon to the center middle side of the hat. Make two small horizontal stitches at the center.

4. Wrap the grosgrain tightly around the hat, overlapping the other end by 1" (2.5cm). Hand-tack with two small, horizontal stitches at the vertical center.

5. Secure the band to the hat in a few other places with a small, vertical hand-tack stitch, each individually tied off from inside the hat. Pull the grosgrain ribbon ⅛" (.8cm) below the rope line before stitching.

TIP: *Avoid stitching at the center front and center back, since an imperfect tack will be most visible in these places.*

6. With the scissors, cut a 2¼" (6cm)-long piece of grosgrain ribbon for the "knot." Fold in both ends ½" (1.3cm). With the pressing iron, flatten the ends.

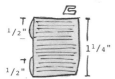

7. Wrap the "knot" around the banding overlap, setting the ½" (1.3cm) bend-back ends behind the banding. With the sewing needle, hand-tack the "knot" closed at all four corners, tying off the knots inside of the hat.

8. Pinch the crown of the hat at the front, bend the brim to an asymmetrical curve or pull it down over your eyes.

Now, have a "knot-ty" time!

We've Got the Pleat:
The Pleated
Ribbon Band

WHAT YOU NEED:

- ❏ Vintage fedora hat
- ❏ 1 yard (1m) of 2¹/₂"(6.4cm)-wide ribbon (any pattern, any content)
- ❏ Pressing iron
- ❏ Pressing board
- ❏ Spray starch

TIP: *If the ribbon is thin and needs extra stiffness to hold the pleats, use spray starch before ironing.*

- ❏ Sewing needle
- ❏ Heavyweight thread (color to match ribbon)
- ❏ Scissors
- ❏ Ruler

Pleats may not be flattering for men's trousers or they may bring back memories (nightmares?) of your old, scratchy Catholic-school uniform, but a pleated ribbon band is a quick, easy way to give a fedora an old-school, couture finish.

HOW TO MAKE THE PLEATED RIBBON BAND:

1. Set the ribbon lengthwise and evenly fold two ¼" (.6cm) deep pleats, centered vertically, to a finished height of 1½" (3.2cm).

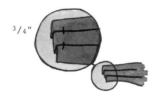

1½"

2. Pinch one end smaller to ¾" (2cm) and handtack closed. With pressing iron, press flat.

¾"

3. At the front side of your fedora, line up the top edge of the ribbon end with the ropeline (where the crown meets the brim). With the sewing needle, hand-tack the pleated end, tying off the knot at the side of the hat.

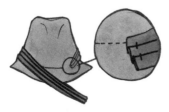

TIP: *To find the front side, put on the hat and make the front edge parallel to the outside edge of your eye.*

4. Wrap the remaining pleated ribbon around the hat, overlapping the long end over the tacked end. With the scissors, cut off the excess ribbon, leaving a 2" (5cm)-long extension.

5. Tuck the extra 2" (5cm) underneath the already-tacked-down end. Hand-tack the tucked end to the hat, hiding the stitches from the outside.

6. Hand-tack the ribbon to secure it in a few places around the hat, hiding the stitches at the inside of the bottom pleat. Before stitching it, pull the bottom edge of the ribbon ⅛" (.3cm) below the ropeline.

Now you've got some sweet pleats!

WHAT YOU NEED:

- ❏ Vintage fedora hat
- ❏ 1 yard (1m) strip of 1" (2.5cm)-wide soft leather (color and texture to complement the fedora)

TIP: *Fabric stores sell flat leather trim (real or fake) by the yard in different colors. Experiment with what looks best on your hat. Softness is important, as it makes it easier to punch holes through the leather.*

- ❏ 1" (2.5cm) metal buckle (with prong)

TIP: *Fabric and trim stores sell buckles in different shapes and materials, so choose one that looks best with your hat. Make sure the center "inside to inside" of the buckle is 1" (2.5cm) in height.*

- ❏ Hole puncher (either a hole puncher that makes mini holes from an office supply store or a craft hole puncher from a craft supply store)
- ❏ Fabric glue (clear Magnatac 809 or white Sobo glue)

TIP: *Let the glue dry for a few minutes after using.*

- ❏ Scissors
- ❏ Fabric pencil

TIP: *Dig an old belt out of your closet and recycle it as trim for your hat . . . or your baby brother's child-sized belt may fit perfectly.*

Back in the olden days, getting in trouble at school often meant not only a meeting with the principal but also with his belt. While those corporal-punishment days are long over, I've discovered a much better use for the belt—this leather belt trim with metal buckle. Don't worry, though, because making it is quick and painless! In fact, it's a cinch!

HOW TO MAKE THE LEATHER BELT TRIM WITH METAL BUCKLE:

1. With the hole puncher, punch a small hole 1½" (3.8cm) from one end of the leather strip. Weave the leather through the buckle and bend back the edge 1" (2.5cm). With the fabric glue, glue the end closed.

2. Place the buckle at the front side of the fedora. With the fabric glue, coat the leather strip and secure it ¼" (.6cm) below the ropeline (where the crown meets the brim).

3. Before gluing the entire leather strip down through the buckle, measure a 4" (10cm) extension from the center of the buckle and cut off the excess. Cut the end into a V-shape.

4. With the fabric pencil, mark the hole through which the prong should go. Then mark two holes on each side of the first mark, spaced 1" (2.5cm) apart. With the hole puncher, punch out the holes.

Now buckle up, sit back, and enjoy the ride!

Below the Belt: The Leather Belt Trim with Metal Buckle

PROJECT

Once Bitten, Twice Shy:
The Snake Band

WHAT YOU NEED:

- ❑ Vintage fedora hat
- ❑ 31"-x-2" (79 x 5cm) strip of black or any color snakeskin-textured vinyl (or use real snakeskin)
- ❑ 2 diamond-shaped 1/2" (1.3cm) long, clear, flat-back crystals
- ❑ 1 1/2" (3.8 cm) length of 1/8" (.3cm)-wide flat red leather trim
- ❑ Fabric pencil
- ❑ Scissors
- ❑ Fabric glue (clear Magnatac 809 or white Sobo glue)

TIP: *Let the glue dry for a few minutes after using.*

Maybe if Adam had been sporting a snake-banded fedora, Eve would have listened to him instead of the evil serpent in the tree, and we could have avoided that whole "downfall of humanity" thing. Oh well! It's not too late for you to reap the benefits of making this reptile-inspired band. It will give your hat a dark side, and make you glad to be a sinner!

HOW TO MAKE THE SNAKE BAND:

1. With the fabric pencil, trace a "snake head" shape onto the back side of the snakeskin-textured fabric. Make the head 1¾" (4.5cm) at the widest point, 3" (7.6cm) in length and 1¼" (3.2cm) wide at the base of the head.

2. Trace the remaining length of the "body" 1¼" (3.2cm) wide. To create the "tail," gradually reduce the width to a ¼" (.6cm) rounded point, starting 8" (20cm) from tail end. With the scissors, cut out the entire "snake."

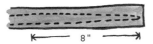

3. Line up the base of the "head" with the brim edge at the front side of the fedora. Leaving the "head" and "tail" unglued, glue the "body" around the hat along the crown/brim seam.

4. Glue the "tail" underneath the "head" at an angle. Then glue the "head" over the "tail."

5. With the fabric glue, glue the crystal "eyes" onto the "head" 1¼" (3.2cm) from the tip.

6. Insert and glue ½" (1.3cm) of the red leather trim underneath the tip of the "snake head." With the scissors, snip out the "fork" at the tip of the tongue.

Now, put on your hat, and snake, rattle, and roll!

TIP: *To make it a diamondback snake, glue crystals into repeating diamond patterns. For a rattlesnake variation, cut the "tail" 5" (13cm) longer, then coil it into a "rosette." Or if you fear deadly snakes, try one of the garden variety—in green snakeskin.*

WHAT YOU NEED:

- ❏ Vintage fedora hat
- ❏ 2 large (1¼" wide x 3¾" long [3.2 x 9.5cm]) feathers
- ❏ 2 small (1" wide x 2¾" long [2.5 x 7cm]) feathers

TIP: *In choosing feather colors, consider a contrasting combination— Large feathers can be a pop color, and the small feathers can be a darker shade of the fedora.*

- ❏ Spray starch
- ❏ Sharpie marker
- ❏ Straight ruler
- ❏ Scissors
- ❏ Fabric glue (clear Magnatac 809 or white Sobo glue)

TIP: *Let the glue dry for a few minutes after using.*

My personal style is so unreal plastic pop sixties that I can't stand to do a feather trim the classic way. I like taking an organic material, like feathers, chemically spraying the life out of it, and cutting it into an unnatural geometric shape. I also like cutting small circles at the top of the feather and shaving the rest down to the quill for a feather lollipop. But that's just me. The beauty is that you can cut this trim in many different shapes. When you get good at this, cut your own monogram by making each feather a letter. Always remember, though, diamond feathers are a girl's best friend!

HOW TO MAKE THE DIAMOND FEATHER TRIM:

1. With the spray starch, evenly spray the front of the feathers, and allow them to fully dry.

TIP: *Spray starch will help you get a clean cut edge with the scissors.*

2. With the scissors, cut a diamond shape out of the larger feathers. Center the side points 1¾" (4.4cm) from the stem and make the width at center 1" (2.5cm) wide.

3. With the scissors, cut a diamond shape out of the small feathers. Secure the side points 1½" (3.8cm) from the top and bottom points and make the centers of the points ¾" (2cm) wide.

4. With the fabric glue, glue the small feather diamonds on top of the large diamonds, lining up the bottom points.

TIP: *When gluing, concentrate on the stem to prevent visible clumps. If you accidentally use too much, let the glue dry and then pick off the hardened pieces with a needle or tweezers.*

5. Glue the feathers to one side of the hat.

Now you know why diamonds are a girl's best friend!

TIP: *A variation of this diamond-shaped feather is to cut off one side to make a triangle.*

Feather Figure: The
Diamond Feather Trim

Join the Fan Club:
The Pleated Fan
Ribbon Trim

WHAT YOU NEED:

- ❑ Vintage fedora hat
- ❑ 2¹/₂" wide x 7" (6 x 18cm)-long length of ribbon (any color, any fabric content)
- ❑ Fabric glue
- ❑ Sewing needle
- ❑ Heavyweight thread (color to match ribbon)

Karl Lagerfeld, designer for the house of Chanel, accessorizes with an elegant fan as protection against cigarette smoke and bad breath. Inspired by both Karl and the Japanese art of origami, I designed this pleated-fan ribbon trim. When you're done, your hat will definitely look fan-tastic!

HOW TO MAKE THE PLEATED FAN RIBBON TRIM:

1. Fold each end of the ribbon back ½" (1.3cm). Using the fabric glue, glue both ends of the ribbon down.

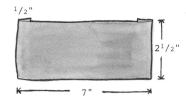

2. Make six accordion folds with the ribbon lengthwise, ½" (1.3cm) deep. Make sure the glued ½" (1.3cm) ends are hidden and set to the back.

3. Pinch the bottom edge and pierce it with the sewing needle ½" (1.3cm) from the bottom edge.

4. Hand-tack the bottom edge closed with stitches secured to the back.

5. Bend the bottom edge of the fan back ½" (1.3cm).

6. With the fedora on your head, mark the fan placement. Hand-tack the base of the fan onto your hat, flaring the fan open. Hand-tack the top folded edge to the hat in a few places, hiding the stitches behind the fan and tying off the knots inside the hat.

Now get ready to fan the flames—that's one hot hat!

FROM HORRIBLE TO FEDORABLE: FAMOUS FEDORA WEARERS

Some men own their look, and make it iconic, when wearing a fedora. Others, like Dick Tracy, look as if they might be trying a bit too hard. Get inspired by these notorious men and the way they wear their trilbys. The key is to figure out what works for you and what doesn't. For instance, feathers may look just right on Bob Dylan but would be so wrong on Freddy Krueger, unless, of course, they were tinged with blood—or shaped like fingernails!

Star	Occupation	Fedora of Choice
Sean Connery as James Bond	The original James Bond, secret agent	White wide-brimmed fedora with dark band—definitely a look that's liscenced to kill.
Bugsy Siegel	Gangster	Dark fedora with black band, a hat befitting this sociopath's sinister soul!
Dick Tracy	Comic-strip detective	Yellow fedora with black band—you're obviously fearless in your use of colors, Dick, but even the color-blind need friends!
Bob Dylan	American singer-songwriter, musician, poet	Big-brimmed with feathers, but we all know he secretly pines for a leopard-skin pillbox hat!
Freddy Krueger	Villain in *Nightmare on Elm Street*	Gray felt fedora with no band, a minimalist look for a boogeyman!
Frank Sinatra	Performer, Rat Pack member	Gray with black band, tilted rakishly atop the head—he does it my way!
Michael Jackson	American musician, singer-songwriter, dancer	Black fedora with black band, a strange choice for the Gloved One, but kids seem to love it!
Clark Kent	Journalist/alter ego of Superman, the superhero	Cream fedora with pinched front and brown band. The hat works better for grounded intellectual Clark than for airborne Superman, whose hair is too good to cover up.
Indiana Jones	Fictional archeologist/adventurer of the Indiana Jones films	In a light brown, wide-brimmed fedora with dark brown band, his fashion future is far from doomed!
Run DMC	Hip-hop group from the eighties	Black fedoras, a look normally reserved for funeral directors and Kid Rock—it's "tricky!"

IDIOM SAVANT: HAT EXPRESSIONS

Talking Through Your Hat

DEFINITION: To talk nonsense or to bullshit.

ORIGIN: This expression was first used in an 1885 interview with a streetcar conductor on the subject of an upcoming uniform change. He is quoted as saying about his supervisors, "Dey're talkin' tru deir hats."

EXAMPLE: I could tell Rose was *talking through her hat* when she called in sick because her coughs sounded fake.

Old Hat

DEFINITION: Out of date or fashion.

ORIGIN: Fashions began to change rapidly in the nineteenth century, and since change was often reflected most dramatically in hats, it is likely that this expression came about during that time.

EXAMPLE: Boho chic was cool last year, but now it's so *old hat*! I wouldn't be caught dead in hippie fringe.

As Mad As a Hatter

DEFINITION: Completely insane; crazy.

ORIGIN: At one time, milliners or hatters actually did go mad from mercury fumes. The chemical was used in the felting process, and the condition was often mistaken for drunkenness. Now the new mercury is spray sizing, which kills brain cells when used without ventilation.

EXAMPLE: My schizophrenic ex-boyfriend Joe is *as mad as a hatter*. I'm so glad that we're not together anymore because I felt like I was dating five guys at the same time.

Hat in Hand

DEFINITION: A gesture of humility. To come "hat in hand" implies deference.

ORIGIN: In feudal times serfs and peasants were required to remove their hats in the presence of members of the upper classes.

EXAMPLE: After my B.F.F. slept with my boyfriend, they both came *hat in hand*, begging for my forgiveness.

Hat Trick

DEFINITION: Three consecutive successes in a game or another endeavor.

ORIGIN: A cricket term, from the traditional prize of a hat to a bowler who dismissed three batsmen in a row.

EXAMPLE: After I won my third round of strip poker, my nude competitors were proof of my *hat trick*.

Hats Off

DEFINITION: An exclamation of kudos or regard.

ORIGIN: Derives from tipping one's hat.

EXAMPLE: *Hats off* to Jason for finally getting into Penn State; we all thought he would just drive around our old high school in his Trans Am, trying to pick up teenage girls for the rest of his life.

Hold on to One's Hat

DEFINITION: A forewarning of imminent danger or excitement.

ORIGIN: Began as a literal warning to horseback riders and car passengers when speed was about to pick up.

EXAMPLE: My inner radar told me to *hold on to my hat* when my boyfriend, Theo, didn't come home on Saturday night and reeked of the perfume Obsession the next morning.

Wearing Many Hats

DEFINITION: Having a multitude of different roles or duties.

ORIGIN: Hats have long been a part of work uniforms. Wearing many hats implies having many jobs.

EXAMPLE: Alex's job at Eugenia Kim requires him to *wear many hats,* from fixing a wooden Bambi's broken left ear before a meeting with Saks to spray-painting graffiti on Pharrell William's custom hat before a *GQ* photo shoot.

Put on One's Thinking Cap

DEFINITION: To consider a grave decision.

ORIGIN: An old courtroom rule required judges to wear a black hat when giving a death sentence.

EXAMPLE: I really had to *put on my thinking cap* when my mom told me to choose between Dior sunglasses or a Louis Vuitton clutch. I mean, one shades me from the sun, and the other holds all my junk. I knew this was something that I'd have to think about long and hard.

Pass the Hat

DEFINITION: To ask for charitable donations.

ORIGIN: Quite literal, as hats are passed as receptacles in church.

EXAMPLE: I really wanted a cashmere hoodie for my toy poodle, Cottonball, but it was astronomically expensive, so I passed the hat to my family and friends and got them all to chip in. Cottonball's fashion welfare is a really important cause!

Chapter 5
A Capped Woman

Growing up as a tomboy prone to hyperphysical activity, I've always embraced the cap as a means of being just one of the boys. With my ponytail threaded through the back loop of a baseball cap, I fearlessly rode bikes, kayaked, played tennis, sailed, rock-climbed, and just ran around constantly as a youth. Nowadays I channel my extreme energy level into the more productive pursuit of hat design, a hands-on activity both physical and mental.

Armed with a steady flow of Diet Coke that I practically mainline, I talk fast and move fast since I have lots of things to take care of each day. I've streamlined my clothing: I usually wear jumpsuits and rely heavily on caps, the most practical and casual of hats. Wearing a cap allows me not to have to wash or do my hair on a daily basis. A cap doesn't look out of place when I'm "wearing my many hats" while running a small business. In it, I do everything from designing, to visiting my factories, to packing the occasional box. It's essentially my "thinking" cap.

Caps are built for the everyday and for everyman (and every-woman). Many styles were originally meant to signify positions of service: conductors, doormen, policemen, newsboys, and chauffeurs all sported them. As a symbol of the working class, the cap became the hat of choice in which to get sweaty and dirty, and blended into the fashion stratosphere to equal casual.

Other caps have their roots in a particular sport: golf, cricket, equestrian, hunting, and, of course, baseball. Baseball, in particular, spawned the most egalitarian and hence American tradition—the baseball cap. First used in 1860 by the Brooklyn Excelsiors baseball team, other teams soon picked up on this hat because the bill kept the sun out of the players' eyes. Before the b-ball cap, players either wore no hat or a cap without a bill.

Eventually, different teams began to individualize this cap with their own logos. Soon, it became a whole new ball game as players and fans alike sported this hat. By the nineties, corporate America—companies like Coca-Cola and McDonald's—began emblazoning their own logos on this hat. Like another American staple, the T-shirt, the baseball cap became a message board to convey the wearer's personal preference for everything from politics, to a favorite band, to a cartoon character. Currently the most common American uniform is a baseball hat, a T-shirt, and a pair of jeans. Today these caps are worn not only by truckers and fast-food workers, but also by hip-hop artists, who wear them backwards like umpires, and by off-duty celebs attempting to duck the paparazzi. Ivy League frat boys curve the bill of their caps to an almost half-circle and run over their caps with their cars just to give them a worn-in look. Even old ladies in Palm Beach are frequently seen speed-walking in their be-sequined b-balls. A cap, with its casual take on American cool, has become the comfort food of headwear for almost everyone.

WEAR IT WELL:
CAPTIVATING

Of course, b-balls look great with jeans and other ultracasual gear like tank tops, hoodies, and sneakers. I like to wear my cap with the brim slightly to the side, with a long pony on the other side to offset the balance. Or you can wear it with two pigtails for a supercute look. This hat looks out of place with vamped-up makeup but seems at home with some bubble-gum pink lip gloss.

Engineer and newsboy caps can take on more glamour, and work with all lengths of hair. Shape a few curls of your short hair toward the face with gel, or wear long hair down or in a French braid. I like newsboy caps best with a face fresh from the country. To achieve this look, give yourself windblown-rosy cheeks with a liquid stain blush. A neutral tweed cap can contrast nicely with a touch of gold shimmer on your eyes, or a well-defined, deep-berry lip. Lately I love channeling the horsey girl with my little velvet newsie paired with a fitted corduroy jacket and tight jeans tucked into long, tall black boots for daytime. An engineer cap in a metallic tweed looks great with a sexy top and jeans— a perfect evening ensemble that doesn't look as if you're trying too hard.

Old Sport:
The Baseball Cap

WHAT YOU NEED:

- ❑ ¹/₂ yard (.5m) of fabric (any color, any fabric content)
- ❑ ¹/₂ yard (.5m) of lining (any color, any fabric content)
- ❑ 12"-x-12" (30.5 x 30.5cm) square of buckram or lightweight cardboard
- ❑ 1 yard (1m) of 1¹/₄" (3.2cm)-wide grosgrain ribbon (any color)
- ❑ Scissors
- ❑ Straight pins
- ❑ Sewing machine
- ❑ All-purpose thread (color to match fabric)
- ❑ Pressing iron
- ❑ Pressing board
- ❑ Fabric pencil
- ❑ Sewing needle

TIP: *This pattern is for a 23" (58cm) size Medium. To adjust for a smaller or larger head, see the Millinery TLC section at the back of the book to learn how to shrink and stretch the inside grosgrain band to accommodate your head size.*

When I was twelve, I designed my first baseball cap, a white cap that I decorated with puffy paint for my grandfather for his sixtieth birthday. On it I "puffy painted" images of his favorite things, such as an Arby's roast beef sandwich (one of his favorite foods), a fish (because he loves fishing), and a baseball bat (evocative of his favorite sport). He never wore it after that day and, thankfully, my design sense has improved since then. Still, the beauty of this simple style is that you can use it as a canvas for any trim or image to make it uniquely yours.

HOW TO MAKE THE BASEBALL CAP:

1. See page 136 for the "baseball cap crown" pattern. Photocopy it, and with the scissors, cut it out to use as your pattern piece.

2. Lay the pattern on the self fabric and cut out six pieces. Repeat with the lining fabric.

3. Pin two pieces of self fabric together, right side to right side. Sew them together along one side edge with a ½" (1.3cm) seam allowance.

4. Pin a third piece to the two sewn-together pieces and sew closed along the side edge.

5. Repeat steps 3 and 4 with the remaining three pieces.

6. Pin together the two half-crown pieces, securing a pin at the top point, and sew closed in a continous stitch with ½" (1.3cm) seam allowance .

TIP: *For a cleaner curve line at all the seams, snip ³/₈" (1cm)-long slits along the seam allowance, spaced ¼" (.6cm) apart. With the pressing iron, open the seams.*

7. Repeat steps 3 to 6 with the lining fabric. Sew the pieces right side to right side, but keep the seam allowances facing out. Set these two pieces aside.

MAKING THE BILL:

8. See page 139 for the "baseball bill" pattern. Photocopy it and with the scissors, cut it out to use as your pattern piece. Lay the "baseball bill" pattern on the buckram (or cardboard). With the fabric pencil, trace the shape onto

the cardboard. Then trace a line ½" (1.3cm) inside the trace line. With the scissors, cut along this inside line.

9.   Lay the pattern piece on the fabric and cut out two pieces.

10. Pin the two bill self fabric pieces together, right side to right side. Sew the outside edges together with a ½" (1.3cm) seam allowance.

TIP: *To bring out the shape of any curved seam, snip ⅜"-(1cm) long slits into the seam allowance, spaced ¼" apart.*

11. Turn the bill inside out and insert the cardboard bill piece, laying cardboard piece above the seam allowance. With the sewing needle, baste the bill closed at the inside curve, with a ½" (1.3cm) seam allowance, securing the cardboard piece as tightly as possible inside the fabric shell.

TIP: *Securing the cardboard piece as tightly as possible inside the fabric shell will give more structure to the bill. Also use it as a "guide line" when pinning the bill to the cap.*

FINISHING THE CAP . . .

12. Layer the self fabric (seam allowance to the inside) over the lining shell (seam allowance to the outside) and sew closed at the bottom edge with a ¼" (.6cm) seam allowance.

13. Center the bill with one vertical crown seam at the center front, pinning the bottom edge of the bill to the shell, with the bill bottom edge ¼" (.6cm) below the shell seam allowance edge (the stitch lines on the bill should match the stitch line on the shell). Sew all layers together over the existing stitchline.

14. Place the grosgrain ribbon over the seam allowance. Line up the top edge of the grosgrain ribbon ⅜" (1cm) above the seam edge, overlapping 1" (2.5cm) at the center back and sew closed. Then pin and cut off the excess ribbon.

15. Turn the bill down and fold the grosgrain ribbon inside the hat. With the pressing iron, press the fold with steam so that the grosgrain ribbon is set ⅛" (.3cm) below the fold edge.

Now, you'll definitely make it to first base!

VARIATION

Get Ciggy with It:
The Snakeskin
Cigarette Trim

WHAT YOU NEED:

- ❏ 1/4" (.6cm) round wood dowel
  (This can be found at any hardware or craft store.)

  QUICK TIP: *In place of a wood dowel, use a pencil, but make sure it has a round, smooth surface.*

- ❏ 1"-x-7/8" (2.5 x 2.2cm) rectangle of light brown textured leather or snakeskin

- ❏ 2 1/8"-x-1" (5.5 x 2.5cm) rectangle of white textured leather or snakeskin

  TIP: *The thinner the leather the better. It is also important for these two leathers to be similar in thickness, as they must be level at the "filter" seam.*

- ❏ 1 round, 1/4" (.6cm)-diameter dusty beige (or red, if you want to be smokin' hot) flatback crystal

- ❏ Craft saw

- ❏ High-grade sandpaper (60 to 80 grade)

- ❏ Wite-Out or white paint pen

- ❏ Fabric glue (clear Magnatac 809 or white Sobo glue)

- ❏ Gold metallic thread

- ❏ Super Glue

- ❏ Computer

- ❏ Computer printer

- ❏ 1 sheet of regular printer paper

- ❏ Scissors

- ❏ UHU glue stick

- ❏ 1" (2.5cm) metal craft pin

It's human nature to want to do the things you're not allowed to do. So right after Mayor Bloomberg banned smoking in all restaurants and bars in New York City, smoking became even cooler because it was forbidden, much the way drinking became glamorous during Prohibition in the 1920s. Especially timely and popular was my invention of this cigarette trim. Even if you're a nonsmoker, there's nothing more luxe than a crystal-flamed snakeskin fag tucked behind your ear and pinned to your cap! This is one cig that won't cause cancer!

HOW TO MAKE THE SNAKESKIN CIGARETTE TRIM:

1. With the craft saw, cut the wood dowel to a 3" (7.6cm) length. Rub the ends against sandpaper to level them off.

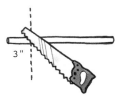

TIP: *However, do not sand off more than 1/8" (.3cm) total, as the leather has already been cut for a 3" (7.6cm) finished dowel.*

2. With Wite-Out, paint both short ends white.

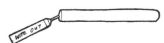

3. With the fabric glue, spread a light, even coat of glue on the back side of the light brown leather piece. Line up the leather piece with the dowel lengthwise and roll up the leather piece around the end of the dowel, allowing a 1/8" (.3cm) overlap. This will be the "filter" end of the "cigarette."

TIP: *Let the glue dry for a few minutes after using.*

TIP: *Wrap the leather as tightly as possible and clean up any glue spots at the overlap edge.*

4. With the fabric glue, spread a light, even coat of glue on the back side of the white leather piece. Line up with the "filter" seam and roll it up lengthwise. Make sure the edges line up exactly.

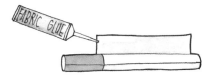

5. At 1/8" (.3cm) below the "filter" seam, tightly wrap gold metallic thread around the "cigarette" five times. Knot off the gold thread at the underside of the overlap seam.

6. With the Super Glue, glue the crystal into the 1/8" (.3cm) gap at the "cigarette" end.

7. Personalize your "cigarette" by printing out your name on white paper in 7-point type in the text font of your choice. With the scissors, cut out the text. With the glue stick, glue the paper into place ⅛" (.3cm) below the wrapped gold metallic thread.

8. Center the "cigarette" over the "filter" seam with the leather overlap edges set to the underside. With a mix of fabric glue and Super Glue, glue the "cigarette" onto the metal craft pin.

9. Now pin the "cigarette" onto your hat at the front side near the crown/brim seam.

Smoke 'em if you got 'em!

THE RULES:
A BAD GIRL'S GUIDE TO HAT ETIQUETTE

There was a time when every man wore a hat, and had to tip it when he saw a lovely lady. After John F. Kennedy stopped wearing hats to major events (like his inauguration) as president, men followed his lead. JFK was single-handedly responsible for the demise of the hat as a staple in men's fashion. Sorry, girls, your guy's Yankees cap doesn't count. Nowadays you're lucky to find a man with enough taste to wear a nice hat.

Hat etiquette for ladies has been a bit more lax, since some hats were pinned securely to one's new 'do or tied with ribbons and would have been awkward to remove in public. If you want to be a "Rules" girl, you need to follow these modern-day hat guidelines:

• **Rule #1**
  Take off your hat when you're eating. It's totally gross to see cock feathers swimming in your soup because you were too lazy to take it off pre-chow.

• **Rule #2**
  When attending a movie, a concert, or a Broadway show, you should take off your hat as a courtesy to the people who don't have front-row tickets. The only exception to this rule is if you happen to have a bald head.

• **Rule #3**
  When attending a funeral, or when your pet Pom dies, or even if you lose your iPod, show some respect and take off your hat. The perfect accessory—a moment of silence.

• **Rule #4**
  If you're on a Roman holiday and have a hankering to see the pope, visit the Vatican and leave your chapeau unchaperoned (that is, show some respect and take off your hat).

• **Rule #5**
  When you're on your way to court (and let's hope it's for jury duty or a parking ticket), be sure to remove your toast cocktail as a sign of deference.

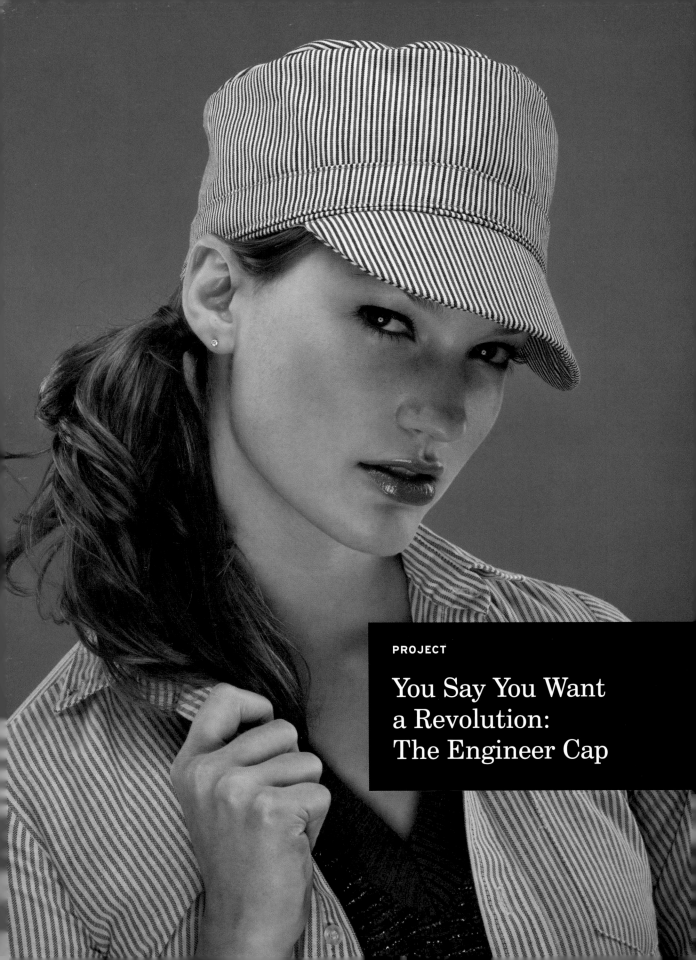

PROJECT

You Say You Want a Revolution: The Engineer Cap

WHAT YOU NEED:

- ❑ ¹/₂ yard (.5cm) of stiff cotton canvas fabric

  TIP: *This style works well with stripes!*

- ❑ ¹/₂ yard (.5m) of lining (any color, any fabric content)

- ❑ 12-x-12" (30.5 x 30.5cm) square of buckram or lightweight cardboard

- ❑ 1 yard of 1¹/₄" (3.2cm)-wide grosgrain ribbon (any color)

- ❑ 1 sheet of 8¹/₂"-x-11" (22 x 28cm) paper

- ❑ Scissors

- ❑ Straight ruler

- ❑ Fabric pencil

- ❑ Straight pins

- ❑ Sewing machine

- ❑ All-purpose thread (color to match fabric)

- ❑ Pressing iron

- ❑ Pressing board

- ❑ Sewing needle

TIP: *This pattern is for a 23" (58cm) size Medium. To adjust for a smaller or larger head, see the Millinery TLC section at the back of the book to learn how to shrink and stretch the inside grosgrain band to accommodate your head size.*

A cap with a cylinder crown is alternately referred to as the engineer cap, the Civil War cap, and the Mao cap. Though its origin is debatable, it seems to be a by-product of revolution: the engineer cap from the Industrial Revolution, the Civil War cap from the American Southerners' revolt, and the Mao cap from the Cultural Revolution. Don't worry, though! You don't need to completely wipe out an entire country replete with thousand of years of civilization to create your own Cultural Revolution. Create a fresh new you by making and wearing this hat!

HOW TO MAKE THE ENGINEER CAP:

1. See page 137 for the "engineer cap/ floppy sun hat crown" pattern piece. Photocopy it and cut out the half oval. Trace it onto a separate sheet of paper that has been folded in half. Then flip the pattern piece along the center fold line and trace the other side. With scissors, cut out the completed oval pattern piece.

2. Lay the paper pattern piece on the self fabric and cut out one piece. Repeat with the lining fabric.

3. With the straight ruler and the fabric pencil, draw a 4¹/₄"-x-24" (11 x 61cm) rectangle on the backside of the fabric. With the scissors, cut it out. Repeat with the lining fabric.

24"

4. Fold the rectangle in half lengthwise, right side to right side. Sew the two short ends together with a ¹/₂" (1.3cm) seam allowance.

5. Unfold it into a cylinder, then pin the circle piece (right side of fabric facing down) to the top edge. Sew the seam closed with a ¹/₂" (1.3cm) seam allowance. Remove the pins and turn the cylinder right side out (so that you cannot see the seam allowance from the outside).

TIP: *For a cleaner curve line at the circle seam, snip ³/₈" (1cm)-long slits along the seam allowance, spaced ¹/₄" (.6cm) apart. With the pressing iron, press open the seams.*

6. Repeat steps 4 and 5 with the lining fabric. Keep the seam allowances facing out. Set these two pieces aside.

4¹/₄"

MAKING THE BILL:

7. See page 141 for the "bill" pattern. Photocopy it and with the scissors, cut it out to use as your pattern piece. Lay the "bill" pattern piece on the cardboard. With the fabric pencil, trace the shape onto the buckram or cardboard. Then with a ruler, trace a line ½" (1.3cm) inside the pattern piece trace line. Cut out one piece along this inside line.

8. Lay the template on the self fabric and cut out two pieces along this inside line.

9. Pin the two bill self fabric pieces together, right side to right side. Sew the outside edges together with a ½" (1.3cm) seam allowance.

TIP: *To bring out the shape of any curved seam, snip ⅜" (1cm)-long slits into the outside curve seam allowance, spaced ¼" (.6cm) apart.*

10. Turn the bill right side out and insert the buckram or cardboard bill piece. With the sewing needle, baste the bill closed at the inside curve, with a ½" (1.3cm) seam allowance, securing the cardboard piece as tightly as possible inside the fabric shell.

TIP: *Securing the cardboard piece as tightly as possible inside the fabric shell will give more structure to the bill. Also use it as a "guide line" when pinning the bill to the cap.*

11. Layer the self fabric (seam allowance to the inside) over the lining (seam allowance to the outside) and sew closed at the bottom edge with a ¼" (.6cm) seam allowance. Turn the vertical seam to the center back.

12. Center the bill at the front center, pinning the bottom edge of the bill to the shell, with the bill bottom edge ¼" (.6cm) below the shell seam allowance edge (the stitch lines on the bill should match the stitch line on the shell). Sew all three layers together with a ¼" (.6cm) seam allowance.

13. Place the grosgrain ribbon over the seam allowance. Line up the top edge of the grosgrain ribbon ⅜" (1cm) above the seam edge, overlapping 1" (2.5cm) at the center back and sew closed. Then pin and cut off the excess ribbon.

14. Turn down the bill and fold the grosgrain ribbon inside the hat. With the pressing iron, press the fold so that the grosgrain ribbon is set ⅛" (.3cm) below the fold edge.

15. With the scissors, cut a 1½"-x-24" (3.8 x 61cm) strip of self fabric—this will be your "band." Fold down ¼" (.6cm) lengthwise from the top and bottom edges, for a finished height of 1" (2.5cm). With the sewing machine, sew an edge stitch at the top and bottom of the band.

16. With the sewing needle, hand-tack the band onto the hat along the bottom edge of the crown, sewing the band seam closed at the center back with a ½" (1.3cm) seam allowance.

Now, you're on track!

TIP: *To make this into a sun visor, make a wider version of the headband (steps 15–16), by cutting a 3"-x-24" (7.6 x 61cm) self fabric piece, and finishing to a height of 2" (5cm). Follow steps 7–10 to make the bill, and sew it under the headband at the bottom edge of center front.*

Newsboy for the Material Girl: The Newsboy

WHAT YOU NEED:

- ❑ 1/2 yard (.5m) of fabric (use a heavyweight cotton canvas, denim, or wool for best results)
- ❑ 1/2 yard (.5m) of lining (any color, any fabric content)
- ❑ 12"-x-12" (30.5 x 30.5cm) square of buckram or lightweight cardboard
- ❑ 1 yard (1m) of 1 1/4" (3.2cm)-wide grosgrain ribbon (any color)
- ❑ 1 1/2" (3.8cm)-wide, dome-shaped, fabric-covered button

TIP: Sewing supply stores have "do-it-yourself" button-covering kits. Choose a size and shape that you like.

- ❑ 1 sheet of 8 1/2"-x-11" (22 x 28cm) paper
- ❑ Scissors
- ❑ Straight pins
- ❑ Sewing machine
- ❑ All-purpose thread (color to match fabric)
- ❑ Pressing iron
- ❑ Pressing board
- ❑ Fabric pencil
- ❑ Sewing needle

TIP: This pattern is for a 23" (58cm) size Medium. To adjust for a smaller or larger head, see the Millinery TLC section at the back of the book to learn how to shrink and stretch the inside grosgrain band to accommodate your head size.

The defining moment for me and the newsboy was the first time I saw the Madonna video for "Borderline." After watching it, I badly wanted a puffy black cap with a big bow in the front—exactly like the one she wore—and to spray-paint graffiti with a rubber-bracelet-laden arm. Years later I finally designed my own newsboy, and, ironically enough, the Material Girl got one for herself! Now you can "get into the groove" of making this cap with these simple steps.

HOW TO MAKE THE NEWSBOY CAP:

1. See page 140 for the "newsboy cap crown" pattern. Enlarge and photocopy it and cut out the half-triangle shape. Trace it onto a separate sheet of paper that is folded in half. Then flip the pattern along the center fold line and trace the other side. With scissors, cut out the completed triangle pattern piece.

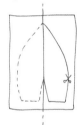

2. Lay the paper pattern on the self fabric and cut out four pieces. Repeat with the lining fabric.

3. Pin two pieces of self fabric together, right side to right side. Sew them together along one side edge with a 1/2" (1.3cm) seam allowance.

4. Repeat step 3 with the remaining two pieces. Pin together the two half-crown pieces, securing a pin at the top point, and sew closed in a continuous stitch with a 1/2" (1.3cm) seam allowance.

5. Sew each dart closed with an edge stitch.

6. Remove the pins and turn the shell right side out (so that you cannot see the seam allowance from the outside).

TIP: For a more finished look, sew top-stitch to both sides of the seam.

TIP: For a cleaner curve line at all the seams, snip 3/8" (1cm)-long slits along the seam allowance at 1/4" (.6cm) intervals. With the pressing iron, press open the seams.

7. Repeat steps 3 to 5 with the lining fabric. Sew the pieces right side to right side, but keep the seam allowances facing out.

8. Place the self fabric (seam allowance to inside) over the lining (seam allowance to outside) and sew closed at the bottom edge with ¼" (.6cm) seam allowance. Turn vertical seam to center back.

9. See page 141 for the "bill" pattern. Photocopy it and with the scissors, cut it out to use as your pattern piece. Lay the "bill" template on the buckram or cardboard. With the fabric pencil, trace the shape onto the cardboard. Then trace a line ½" (1.3cm) inside the trace line. Cut out one piece along this inside line.

10. Lay the pattern piece on the self fabric and cut out two pieces.

11. Pin the two bill self fabric pieces together, right side to right side. Sew the outside edges together with a ½" (1.3cm) seam allowance.

TIP: *To bring out the shape of any curved seam, snip ⅜" (1cm)-long slits into the outside curve seam allowance, spaced ¼" (.6cm) apart.*

12. Turn the bill right side out and insert the cardboard bill piece. With the sewing needle, baste the bill closed at the inside curve, with a ½" (1.3cm) seam allowance, securing the cardboard piece as tightly as possible inside the fabric shell.

TIP: *Securing the cardboard piece as tightly as possible inside the fabric shell will give more structure to the bill. Also use the cardboard as a "guide line" when pinning the bill to the cap.*

13. Cut a 2½"-x-24" (6.4 x 61cm) strip of fabric—this will be your headband. Fold down in half lengthwise to 1¼" (3.2cm) and press the fold with pressing iron and steam.

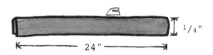

14. Set and pin the folded headband over the bottom edge of the crown shell, lining up all raw edges. Sew all three layers together with ¼" (.6cm) seam allowance.

15. Turn the hat upside down and flip up the headband (1" [2.5cm] finished). Pin the bill to the front center, with raw edge of bill set ½" (1.3cm) below the headband folded edge (stitch line on bill should match to headband folded edge). Set pins to the outside of hat.

16. Overlap the grosgrain ribbon to the inside, ⅛" (.3cm) below headband folded edge. Pin and sew all three layers together with ⅛" (.3cm) topstitch. Allow 1" (2.5cm) overlap at center back and cut off excess ribbon.

17. Then with the sewing needle, sew the button onto the top of the crown. With the fabric-covering button kit, cover the button with the leftover self fabric.

Get ready to make some headlines, newsgirl!

Chapter 6
The Prodigal Sun Hat

Even a workaholic like me needs to take a break every once in a while. On breaks from hat design, I vacation best in the sun. It helps me rejuice, relax, and get a fresh perspective so I can stay creative. It brings me back to the carefree summer days of my youth spent getting brown by the pool morning to evening. Back then I would pay little heed to my father, a cancer doctor, calling after me to wear sunscreen. Now I realize that I need to take better care of myself. There are the threats of wrinkles, sunburn, ruining a good dye job, and, of course, cancer. So when I sunbathe, I wear SPF 30, sunglasses, and a big sun hat.

As early as the nineteenth century, when folks first started going to the beach just for the fun of it, straw hats were linked with the seaside. These hats became the symbol of outdoor life, freedom, and informality—that is, vacation. The first American straw sun hat was made in 1798 by Betsy Metcalfe, a fourteen-year-old girl, who copied an English straw bonnet that she couldn't afford. Her hat was so well received that she got many orders for her fashionable straw hats. Soon afterwards, the straw hat industry took off. (If she can do it, so can you, girl!)

Because they are large, sun hats put you in your own space and therefore offer a different kind of protection. When you go to a party wearing a sun hat, you look mysterious and diva-like rather than super-approachable. Celebs like it for this reason, and because this chapeau is very camera-friendly. After all, a big hat doesn't allow much room for anyone else in the picture. Think Jennifer Lopez and the iconic, camel floppy hat with a gold chain that I made for her.

The sun hat can transform you into a rich hippie à la Talitha Getty, or, with large shades, a glamour girl on holiday. During the 1960s, this hat came to embody movie star sophistication as actresses began wearing sun hats both on- and offscreen. Catherine Deneuve, Julie Christie, and Faye Dunaway donned them in films and on holiday. Brigitte Bardot, the French actress and sex symbol of the decade, was frequently spotted in St. Tropez, playground for the rich and famous, wearing nothing but a bikini and a floppy sun hat. No longer worn just to shade us from the sun, the sun hat, which came to encompass all big-brimmed hats, developed into a fashion accessory both on and off the beach.

Shaped like daisies, sun hats were the perfect emblem of the innocence and youth of the 1960s. While promoting peace, love, and happiness, the flower children wore floppy hats to protect against the sun. Janis Joplin, a folk singer and free-loving symbol of those times, frequently decked herself out in floppy sun hats festooned with feathers while belting out songs like "Summertime" in her trademark husky voice.

Cut to the darker decade of the 1970s, when the kids became a little war-embittered and graduated to some seriously hard drugs and partying. The sleek, sharp-cut pantsuits that mirrored the hard edge of the disco era looked great when topped off with these big, dramatic hats. This resort staple soon came to embody urban sophistication as well. Appropriately enough, party girl Bianca Jagger wore a wide-brimmed white sun hat with matching white pantsuit both for her nights out at Studio 54 (*the* place to be and be seen) and for her 1971 wedding to Mick Jagger in St. Tropez.

Maybe not all of us can afford to vacay at a playboy's paradise or sail away on a multimillionaire's yacht. But even if you're just hanging out in the kiddie pool in your own backyard, you'll still feel like a diva in a sun hat.

WEAR IT WELL: CALIFORNIA DREAMING

A sun hat looks stunning with long, California girl beach hair streaming over the shoulders. You can also pull hair into two loose braids and leave the ends unbound for a glamorous hippie look. Let your skin go bare, save for a sweep of bronzer. You wouldn't wear foundation or powder on the beach, and the hat's large brim casts a flattering shadow that makes imperfections less noticeable anyway.

If your hair is shorter, slick it back and fasten it at the nape; let the silhouette be all about the big, floppy hat. For a film-star-on-holiday look, skip the bronzer, and go for porcelain skin instead; then paint on an immaculate red lip.

The shape of the sun hat is super flattering for almost every face shape. The big brim acts as a frame for the wearer, so your face always looks ten pounds thinner with one on. Sun hats look movie star dramatic when one side of the brim covers part of your face. If you want to go more bohemian, make sure the sun fades your hat a little. Also, playing on the beach will beat it up a bit.

Of course, sun hats look great with bikini tops, sarongs, short-shorts, and sundresses. Just don't go over-boho by pairing a frayed-edge straw hat with fringed cutoffs. Instead, wear your straw cowboy with a floral prairie girl dress à la Laura Ingalls Wilder. For evening, you can do the seventies-sophisticate pantsuit thing by wearing a suit in a light fabric and color. Don't wear anything underneath the jacket, and go for the gold with a deep V of cleavage. Then accessorize with metallic, high-heeled sandals and you're ready to party!

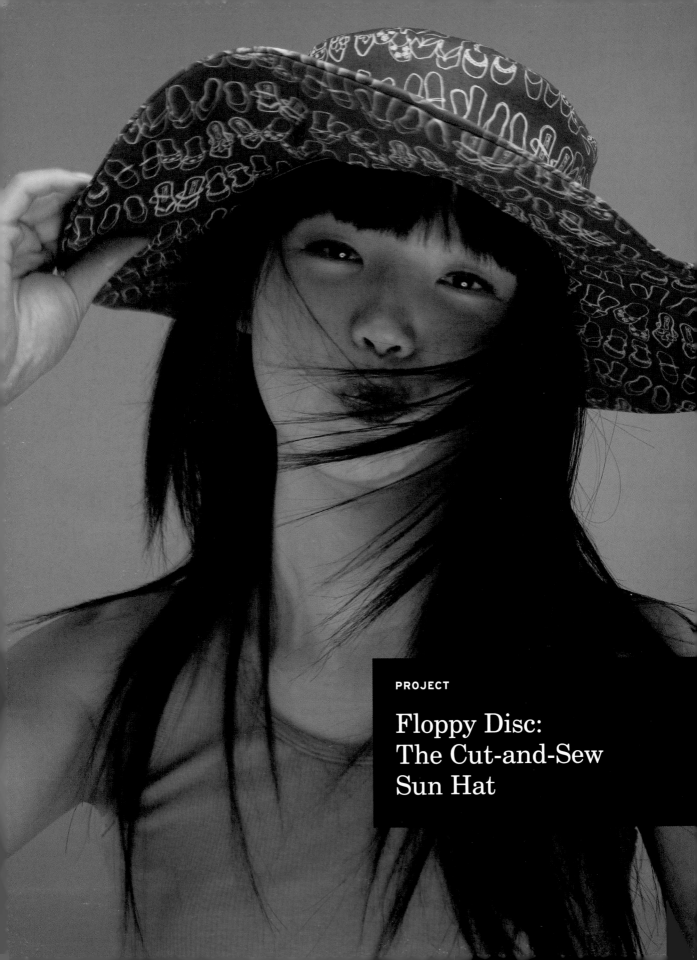

Floppy Disc:
The Cut-and-Sew
Sun Hat

WHAT YOU NEED:

- [ ] 1 yard (1m) of fabric (any color, any fabric content)
- [ ] ¹/₂ yard (.5m) of lining (any color, any fabric content)
- [ ] 30"-x-30" (76 x 76cm) sheet of buckram
- [ ] 1 yard of 1¹/₄" (3.2cm)-wide grosgrain ribbon (any color)
- [ ] Scissors
- [ ] 1 sheet of 8¹/₂" x 11" (22 x 28cm) paper
- [ ] Straight ruler
- [ ] Fabric pencil
- [ ] Sewing machine
- [ ] All-purpose thread (color to match fabric)
- [ ] Straight pins
- [ ] Pressing iron
- [ ] Pressing board
- [ ] Compass

TIP: *This pattern is for a 23" (58cm) size Medium. To adjust for a smaller or larger head, see the Millinery TLC section in the back of the book to learn how to shrink and stretch the inside grosgrain band to accommodate your head size.*

A big floppy hat is perfect for concealing your most recent cosmetic surgery, when you're not quite ready to debut the new nipped-and-tucked you (read: nose job). I'm pretty sure this is the reason I sell a lot of sun hats in Beverly Hills. Even if you don't succumb to the scalpel, you can still pretend to play coy with the paparazzi by wearing this fab hat!

HOW TO MAKE THE CUT-AND-SEW SUN HAT:

1. See page 137 for the "engineer cap/ floppy sunhat crown" pattern. Photocopy it and cut out the half oval. Trace it onto a separate sheet of paper that is folded in half. Then flip the pattern along the center fold line and trace the other side. With scissors, cut out the completed oval pattern.

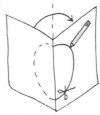

TIP: *Crown shapes can be interchangeable. Make another version of the floppy sun hat with the six-piece crown of the Baseball Cap from Chapter 5!*

2. Lay the pattern on the self fabric and cut out one piece. Repeat with the lining fabric.

3. With the ruler and the fabric pencil, draw a 4¹/₄"-x-24" (11 x 61cm) rectangle on the self fabric. With the scissors, cut it out. Repeat with the lining fabric.

4¹/₄"

24"

4. Fold the rectangle in half lengthwise, right side to right side. Sew the two short ends together with a ¹/₂" (1.3cm) seam allowance.

5. Unfold it into a cylinder, then pin the circle edge (right side facing down) to the top edge. Sew the seam closed with a ¹/₂" (1.3cm) seam allowance. Remove the pins and turn the cylinder right side out (so that you cannot see the seam allowance from the outside).

TIP: *For a cleaner curve line at the circle seam, snip ³/₈" (1cm)-long slits along the seam allowance at ¹/₄" (.6cm) intervals. With the pressing iron, press open the seams.*

TIP: *For a more finished look, sew topstitch to both sides of the seam.*

6. Repeat steps 4 and 5 with the lining fabric. Sew the two short ends together, right side to right side, but keep the seam allowances facing out. Set these two pieces aside.

7. With the compass and the fabric pencil, draw two 3⅛" (8cm)-radius circles (6¼" [16cm] diameter) on the self fabric. Then trace a 5" (13cm) border around the circle. With the scissors, cut out these two "rings"—this will be your brim.

8. With the compass and the fabric pencil, draw a 3⅝" (9cm)-radius circle (7¼" [18.5cm] diameter) on the buckram. Then trace a 4" (10cm) border around the circle. With the scissors, cut out the "ring"—this will be the brim reinforcement.

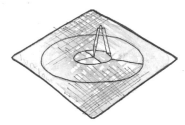

9. Pin the two self fabric "rings" together, right side to right side. Sew the outside edges together with a ½" (1.3cm) seam allowance. After sewing the seam, clip ⅜" (1cm)-long slits in the seam allowance (as earlier in step 5), spaced ¼" (.6cm) apart.

10. Turn the brim right side out. With the pressing iron, press the outside seam with steam to flatten edge. Insert the buckram ring inside the fabric shell and press it tightly to the edge of the seam.

TIP: *As a stitching detail option, secure the curve shape at the outside brim edge with a topstitch, through all of the layers.*

11. Turn the self/lining crown shell upside down on its top. Line up the inside circle of the brim with it. Pin and sew all three layers together with a ¼" (.6cm) seam allowance.

12. Keeping the hat turned upside down, overlap the grosgrain ribbon over the seam allowance and pin. Line up the top edge of the grosgrain ribbon ⅜" (1cm) below the seam allowance edge, overlapping 1" (2.5cm) at the center back and stitch. Cut off the excess ribbon.

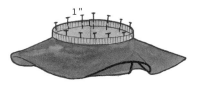

13. Turn the brim down and fold the grosgrain inside the hat. With the pressing iron, press with steam so that the grosgrain ribbon is set ⅛" (.3cm) below the folded edge.

14. With the pressing iron, steam one side of the front brim while pulling it down for an asymmetrical look. Press brim edge to flatten seam.

Now you're ready for some fun in the sun!

Urbane Cowboy:
The Straw Cowboy Hat

WHAT YOU NEED:

- ❏ 1 straw hat with round crown
- ❏ 5 yards (5m) of ⅛" (.3cm) flat leather cording (color should complement straw hat color)

  TIP: *If you cannot find leather cording, any ⅛" (.3cm) ribbon will work.*

- ❏ ¼" (.6cm) metal grommet kit (Fabric stores have kits that include grommets and tool attachments.)
- ❏ Sewing needle
- ❏ Heavyweight thread (any color)
- ❏ Spray sizing (This is an aerosol chemical spray specific to millinery that will stiffen and hold the straw in shape.)
- ❏ Scissors
- ❏ Clear tape
- ❏ Fabric glue (clear Magnatac 809 or white Sobo glue)

  TIP: *Let the glue dry for a few minutes after using.*

- ❏ Straight pins

Back in the good ole frontier days, the cowboy hat was worn to protect from the sun, the rain, and the wind. Cowboys also used them to fan a fire quickly, whip a horse, and wave to distant riders. Subtle nuances in shape and style let other riders know details of the wearer's geographical background. (Different dents in the crown and tilts of the brim signified whether a man was from the northern regions of Nevada or the wind-whipped ranges of the Rockies.) This hat was originally worn by rugged individuals who carved out a life taming beasts and a new frontier. I just like them because they look cool with jeans, make me look tough, and give my round face a natural face-lift!

HOW TO MAKE THE STRAW COWBOY HAT:

1. With the thumb, index, and middle fingers, make a three-finger pinch at the top middle center of the hat's crown. Your index finger will create the center **V** indent.

2. With the double-threaded sewing needle, pierce into the holes of the straw, ½" (1.3cm) below the top edge and perpendicular to the two "hills" at the top center of the crown. Cinch tightly and secure with a knot.

TIP: *Pull and secure the knot a little tighter than you want visually, as the thread may loosen a little after knotting.*

3. Turn the hat upside down. With the spray sizing, spray the inside crown. Set the hat aside to dry right side up. For best results, let it dry overnight, but otherwise for at least 1 hour.

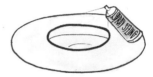

TIP: *It is very important to use spray sizing in a well-ventilated area, preferably outside. Read all the instructions and warnings on the back of the can before using.*

4. While the spray sizing is drying, with the scissors, cut three 1-yard (1m) strips of leather cording. With the clear tape, tape down the strips at one end to any surface and braid them evenly.

COWGIRL HALL OF FAME

Sharpshooter Annie Oakley was the original cowboy-hat-wearing woman back in the nineteenth century, but you don't have to wield a rifle to put one on. Get inspired by these famous *chicas*!

- **Dallas Cowboys cheerleaders (1970s)** sported white cowboy hats, starting the trend of girls wearing cowboy hats.
- **Catherine Bach in *The Dukes of Hazzard* TV show (1979–1985),** as Daisy Duke, modeled a brown felt version with her signature denim cut-offs.
- **Debra Winger in *Urban Cowboy* (1980)** donned a natural straw cowboy and also a high-crowned black felt number that matched John Travolta's.
- **Susan Sarandon in *Thelma & Louise* (1991)** wore a straw cowboy hat with jeans, a white tank top, and a tanned face.
- **Uma Thurman in *Even Cowgirls Get the Blues* (1993)** wore a beige cowboy boho-style with a caramel suede jacket.
- **Madonna in her "Music" video (2000)** had on a white cowboy hat with gold crystal detailing and a matching white pimp coat.

5. With the fabric glue, glue the braided trim to the headsize (where the crown meets the brim), securing the seam at either side (it will eventually be covered up by the brim), and cut off the excess cording.

TIP: *For a more permanent effect, hand-tack the braided trim to the straw in a few places, tying off each individual knot from the inside of the hat.*

6. Turn the hat upside down and bend the side brims down toward the crown at the side center, making sure the curves are parallel to each other. With the straight pins, pin the side brims to the crown.

7. With the grommet kit, set two metal grommets through the brim and crown (two layers), 1" (2.5cm) above the headsize and ½" (1.3cm) from the brim edge. Space the two grommets ¼" (.6cm) from each other. Repeat on the other side center.

TIP: *If your straw hat has an open-weave pattern, skip the grommets and lace the cording directly into the open spaces of the hat.*

8. With the scissors, cut the remaining cording into two 24" (61cm)-long strips and weave them in and out of the metal grommets on both sides. Tie them in a bow on the outside of the hat.

Now you're ready to ride 'em, cowboy.

TIP: *For an even more boho look, fray the brim edge by cutting off the finished edge and pulling apart the weave with your thumbs. The more uneven the fray, the more bohemian the look.*

Call Me Scarf-Face:
The Silk Scarf Trim
for a Sun Hat

WHAT YOU NEED:

- [ ] 1 straw hat
- [ ] 2 yards (2m) of printed silk fabric
    QUICK TIP: *Got a favorite silk scarf that is long and skinny? Skip to step 5 and go straight to setting the grommets.*
- [ ] $1/2$" (1.3cm) or $3/4$" (1.9cm) metal grommet kit (Fabric stores have kits that include grommets and tool attachment.)
- [ ] 1 roll of 45" (114cm)-wide white paper (This is sold in rolls at art supply stores.)
- [ ] Yardstick
- [ ] Pencil
- [ ] Scissors
- [ ] Straight pins

I so coveted Audrey Hepburn's big black Givenchy-designed sun hat with white silk scarf sash in *Breakfast at Tiffany's*. The hat made her look elegant, even when she was hung over and visiting her friend in prison. After watching that film, I designed a slightly more resort version for myself. To do a quick movie star makeover, you can use your designer Pucci or Hermès silk scarf, or even your 50-cent vintage store find. Don't forget your big black sunglasses!

HOW TO MAKE THE SILK SCARF TRIM FOR A SUN HAT:

1. With the yardstick and the pencil, measure and cut two pieces of paper from the roll, each 2 yards (2m) long. Then layer 2 yards (2m) of fabric on top of the other piece of paper and set them aside.

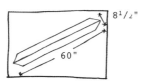

2. With the yardstick and the pencil, draw a rectangle at a 45-degree angle on a piece of paper 8½" (22cm) wide and 60" (152cm) long, shaping the ends into points at the center.

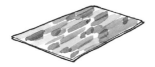

3. Layer this template over the fabric and paper. Secure in place with pins pushed inside and outside of the rectangle, through all three layers.

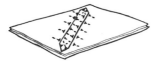

4. With the scissors, cut out the rectangle through all three layers. Unpin it and set it aside.

TIP: *The fabric has a tendency to move around when being cut on the bias, which is why we are securing it in place with paper and pins. Cut slowly and surely, as we will keep the edges raw and want clean cut lines.*

5. With the grommet kit, set one metal grommet through the brim at the side center, ½" (1.3cm) below the rope line. Repeat on the other side center.

6. Weave the fabric strip in one grommet, drape it around the front brim, then weave it out of the other grommet.

Tie the fabric strip behind your neck, put on some sunglasses, and you'll look as smooth as silk!

Here's where you'll find some useful resources and tips, along with interesting semi-relevant tidbits of info—from how to care for your hat (which, in my opinion, should be treated like a precious child) to a glossary of sewing and hat terminology to guidance on where you can find the materials you're going to need to make the hats in this book.

MILLINERY TLC: CARING FOR YOUR HAT

Your hat will give back to you what you give to it, so take good care of your special chapeau!

STAINS ON FELT HATS

For felt hats, first try to sand your beauty with a really fine sandpaper (80 to 120 grade), depending on the level of damage. If your stain is stubborn, apply steam and try to pick it out like a blackhead, using a straight pin or a soft brush. Think of this as a facial for your hat!

STAINS ON CUT-AND-SEW HATS

Dirty cut-and-sew hats should be taken to the dry cleaners, especially if the hats are made with buckram. You can hand-wash hats without buckram or the silk scarf you made for the sun hat yourself. However, it's important to let all cut-and-sew hats dry in their own time. Drying your chapeaux in the dryer could shrink them, wrinkle the fabric near the seams, or fade the brilliant colors over time.

UPKEEP FOR ALL HATS

It's also a good idea to dust your hat occasionally with a soft brush. And for darker colors, a lint brush or even double-sided tape works wonders!

TO MAKE YOUR HAT'S HEAD SIZE SMALLER

In case you've made yourself a new hat and your friend who has a pea-head keeps eyeing your original, you have a few options:

• You can wet the grosgrain ribbon and it will dry tighter overnight. For faster results and a smaller head size, stick the hat near the radiator.

• You can pinch and hand-tack the grosgrain ribbon at both the left center and right center to tighten the ribbon.

• If you're OCD and can't sleep at night unless everything is your idea of perfect, you can sew in another grosgrain ribbon atop the existing one for a sleek, clean look.

TO MAKE YOUR HAT'S HEAD SIZE BIGGER

If you want to stretch your hat up to ¾" (2cm), do it yourself with a little patience and steam. Apply steam around the rope line several times non-stop. Do not be afraid, as steam can never damage a felt hat (unless it's a card-carrying member of your vintage collection). Once you've loosened up the fibers, hand-stretch your hat by carefully pulling it outward from all angles so as not to warp its shape. Don't be too rough though; you wouldn't want to have to make it smaller if you stretched it too big.

KEEPING ITS SHAPE

If your felt feels limp after a season, simply pull out that can of spray sizing you bought when you made it and stiffen that sucker back up again. If your B.F.F. sits on your hat in the back of your boyfriend's 'Vette (which is a terrible place to store your hat, by the way), all it takes is some steam and gentle hand-blocking. Steam will soften the fibers and immediately bring it back to life. You'll have those creases fixed quicker than you can spread warm butter on Grandma's Saturday morning biscuits!

Don't ever wear your hat in the rain—unless it's the rain hat (see the tip on page 34) you made, of course! If it starts to rain while you're trotting

about, take off your hat quickly; otherwise you'll ruin its shape. Once you get home, you can dry it on low with your blow dryer. But you don't want it so dry that it becomes brittle either—that's just as bad as leaving it in the sun!

STORAGE

A hat box is a wise investment. It only takes a few moments of your time to pack up your hat, but this will ensure a lifetime of wear. You can even stack hats with similar crowns on top of each other to maximize your storage space. However, if your chapeau is in season and you know you'll be wearing it frequently, you can hang it on a hook or coatrack for safekeeping and easy access. If you can't even find the time to acquire a hat box, you can at least stuff the crown with paper and store the hat in a bag to protect it from the elements and from being your mini-Maltese's next chew toy.

If you're on tour with the band, cruising in Cozumel, or any place you want to take off your hat, be sure to put your hat on a soft surface when possible. If the brim of your hat slants down, make sure you let the slant hang off the surface when you set down the hat. Placing it on a hard surface will warp the brim over time.

ANATOMY OF A HAT

1. Crown

2. Center Front—This is like north on the compass; it's a good place from which to measure. Don't hand-tack your ribbon here, as it will look really obvious.

3. Rope Line/Headsize

4. Front Side—This is approximately at 1:30 from the Center Front. It's a good place to put a spot trim, as it is more photogenic than the true Side since you can see both the hat trim and your face at the same time in this position.

5. Brim

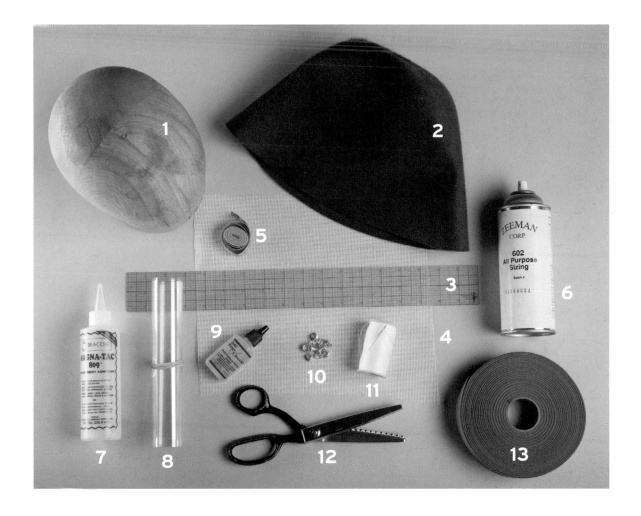

ALL I WANT FOR CHRISTMAS: BASIC MILLINERY SUPPLY CHART

1. Balsa Block
2. Felt Hood
3. Straight Ruler
4. Buckram
5. Tape Measure
6. Spray Sizing
7. Magnatac 809 glue
8. Plastic Sheeting (rolled up)
9. Fray Check glue
10. Grommets
11. Needle and Thread
12. Pinking Shears
13. Roll of Grosgrain Ribbon

MOTHER PLUCKER: A FEATHER GUIDE

1. **Burnt herl**

These are feathers that were once fuzzy but have been through an acid wash and are now just the spines of the plume they once were! They are really good glued onto a headband if you want to make an East London punk Mohawk!

2. **Rooster tail feathers**

Small, skinny, and pointed, these feathers are most commonly found in boas. Take two, add to your fedora, and call me in the morning.

3. **Pheasant feather pad**

This is the oh-so-pleasant natural pheasant. Use this on the full-feathered cloche—it's a notch up from a regular hackle pad, as the pattern will give your hat added luxe. Or try just adding one to the side of your fedora.

4. **Ostrich spines**

These feathers have been shaved and dyed to this bone color. You can really make some abstract designs with these babies!

5. **Natural goose feather**

This feather looks great against a natural-colored fedora for a real men's-tailored look.

6. **Strung undyed hackle feathers**

These feathers look great glued under the brim of a cloche or as a fan on a cocktail hat.

7. **Tiger-stripe rooster pad**

These pads come in a variety of colors and work well for the animal-print lover.

8. **Baby duck feathers**

They come in all these cute colors and are great for accents—they are the least showy feathers if you want to make a hat that's subtle!

9. **Turkey feathers**

This is turkey plumage strung together to give you an idea of the different colors you can buy. These particular ones are white with the tips dyed black. Add these to a headband all around to go for a Pocahontas/debutante tiara.

10. **Ostrich plume**

Basically, it's just a huge feather à la the Three Musketeers. You could cut this into cool shapes, style and curl it as you would your hair, or just tack it on your hat for a real pimptress look. You can also place one in the front of your cloche for an Erte-inspired flapper look.

11. **Teardrop/burnt herl feather combo**

This is a combination of teardrop and burnt herl feathers on a tape. Feathers that are arranged together are great because they are like flower arrangements, only more luxe! Or stick this combo on a headband and that's pretty much all you need in order to feel like Holly Golightly!

12. **Rooster feathers**

Another example of interesting premade trims that you can find while shopping. This feather looks kind of like a bird's wing, so you can cover a mini-Styrofoam ball with feathers and add a beak to put a bird on your cloche.

13. **Peacock feather**

This is my favorite pad. The colors in the feathers are so vibrant and include shades of greens, blues, and browns. Stick one on a barrette, or use it to make your peacock trim. It's a real eye-opener!

14. **Hackle/pheasant feather pad combo**

This shows you how sometimes feathers that were once boring can be combined and be fun again. These are the feathers you use to make the "butterfly" trim.

15. **Biot bundle**

These are long and skinny, and are what I used for the "cucumber" on the Sushi Cocktail.

16. **Teardrop or cock feathers**

These are great accent feathers that are shaped like a spoon. You can put these behind a silk flower or any trim for a more explosive look. These are the feathers you use for the wedding veil.

17. **Plumage feathers in a circle**

This is an example of something unique you can find while you're doing your feather shopping. You can just stick this on the side of your hat—instant added attention.

BIG WORDS YOU SHOULD KNOW: THE GLOSSARY

balsa block: A wooden form in the shape of a head used as a mold for shaping.

baste stitch: A hand-sewing technique of loosely joining fabric using large stitches.

bias: The direction of fabric diagonal to straight grain and cross grain.

blocking: The process of molding a hat shape with heat and moisture.

boucle: A woven or knitted fabric with a knotty or looped texture.

brim: The rim or edge of a hat that protrudes from the crown.

buckram: A coated mesh used to give shape or to reinforce. Can be blocked or sewn.

chapeau, (pl. chapeaux): The French word for "hat."

cross grain: The direction of fabric perpendicular to the selvedge edge.

crown: The top section of a hat that covers the crown of the head.

dart: A V-shape fold or cutout in pattern piece, tapering to one end, used to shape flat fabric to a contoured shape when sewn.

dowel: A cylindrical wooden rod that can be cut to size.

fabric pencil: A special type of pencil used to mark fabric.

felt: A cloth made from wool or fur that is compacted (i.e., felted) by pressing with heat and moisture.

fusible: An iron-on featherweight interfacing that adds body and shape when applied to the back side of fabric.

gather: A method of pulling or cinching fabric together to create fullness.

grommet: A metal ring used to create a metal-reinforced hole in a fabric. A two-piece construction requiring a tool to apply through fabric.

grosgrain: A specific type of tightly woven ribbon with a ribbed texture.

hand-tack: A hand-sewing method where stitches are hidden from the outside.

head size: A millinery term that refers to head circumference.

hood: A roughly shaped cone of felt or straw before it is blocked into a hat shape.

pinking shears: A special type of scissor with a decorative zigzag cut line. This tool prevents fraying on delicate fabrics.

pique: A tightly woven fabric with raised waffle pattern.

polyfill: A synthetic material used as inside stuffing.

rope line: The line where the crown meets the brim of hat. Specific to felt or straw blocked hats.

seam allowance: The remaining measurement of fabric left after sewing seam.

seersucker: A puckered, light cotton fabric that is usually striped.

self: The fabric from which the hat is made.

selvedge: The edge of raw fabric that does not fray.

shantung: A heavy silk fabric with a rough textured surface.

spray starch: A household aerosol spray used to stiffen fabrics when used with pressing iron.

straight grain: The direction of fabric parallel to selvedge edge.

topstitch: A decorative row of stitching, set at the edge of a seam line or finished edge.

tulle: A stiff netting used for veils.

IN A MATERIAL WORLD: RESOURCES AND SUPPLIES

You should be able to find all the materials you need to make the hats and trims in this book by riffling through your craft closet, tool box, and/or junk drawer. If you can't find what you're looking for even after hitting up the garage and your parent's attic, a trip to your local arts & craft store, fabric store, or mega mall may be in your immediate future. The list below will help you find any of the items you may need to complete the projects in the book. You can go to the company's website to locate the store nearest you or order directly online, or call to place an order using the numbers listed below.

FABRIC SOURCES

For bouclé, cotton prints, vinyls, silks, leathers, and other fabrics, try:

- Your local fabricstore, or there's probably a Michaels or a Jo-Ann Fabrics near you. Their web sites are **michaels.com** and **joann.com**.
- **moodfabrics.com** (Mood Fabrics) will send swatches according to your fabric needs and tastes. Mood is my favorite fabric store, so if you're in New York City, it's a one-stop source of inspiration, and the prices are great! If you aren't up for a jaunt in the city, you can order over the phone at (212) 730-5003.
- **bandjfabrics.com** (B & J Fabrics)is awesome if you want really luxe, hard-to-find fabrics or interesting cotton prints. They're based in New York City; if you can't go to the store, email them at info@bandjfabrics.com. They will hand cut samples to you.
- **leatherimpact.com** (Leather Impact)has leather skins, leather trims, snake-skins, and almost all other exotics. And the people who work there are really nice! You may also pick your swatch online and call to place an order at (212) 302-2332.

TRIMMING AND NOTIONS

For trimmings such as satin ribbon, feathers, fabric flowers, leather trim, buttons, and buckles, visit:

- Your local trim supply store.
- **mjtrim.com** (M&J Trimmings) is the most comprehensive store for all your trimming needs.
- **tohoshojiny.com** (Toho Shoji N.Y.) for beads and crystals. When I was trying to make mice out of pearls, this was the only store in town that had flat-backed, teardrop-shaped pearls.
- **zuckerfeather.com** (Zucker Feather Products) for feathers.

MILLINERY SUPPLIES

For buckram, millinery thread, spray sizing, felt and straw hoods, and balsa blocks, try:

- California Millinery Supply doesn't have a web site, but you can call and order a catalog at (212)622-8746; they're pretty comprehensive.
- **judithm.com** (Judith M.) has everything listed above, and the prices are reasonable.
- **metropolitanimpex.com** (Metropolitan) has buckram frames, plastic headbands, and cocktail straps.

SEWING NOTIONS

For thread, needles, pinking shears, fabric pencils, and grommet kits, try:

- Your local notions store, or Jo-Ann Fabrics, if there is a store in your area.
- **atlantathread.com** (Atlanta Thread & Supply Company) is the best site for supplies. I personally love this site.
- **steinlaufandstoller.com** (Steinlauf and Stoller), which sells buckram too! Find what you need online and call (877) 869-0321 to place your order.

ARTS & CRAFT MATERIALS

For grommets, beads, crystals, headbands, and wire, just stop by:

- Your neighborhood art and crafts store.
- **michaels.com** (Michaels)
- **pearlpaint.com** (Pearl) is a fabulous discount art supply outlet.

OFFICE SUPPLIES

For supplies such as a metal hole puncher, compass, straight ruler, and pushpins, check out:

- Your local office supply store.
- **staples.com** (Staples)
- **officedepot.com** (Office Depot)

HARDWARE EQUIPMENT

For supplies such as a craft saw and sandpaper, go to:

- Your local hardware store.
- **homedepot.com** (Home Depot) is a great web site for your hardware needs.

The following templates and patterns accompany the projects
from all of the previous chapters. Simply trace the template or pattern onto a piece of
paper and, where indicated, enlarge using a photocopier.

TOAST COCKTAIL HAT TEMPLATE
(USE AT 100%)
Project instructions can be found on page 66.

HELLO KITTY COCKTAIL HAT TEMPLATE
(USE AT 100%)
Project instructions can be found on page 54.

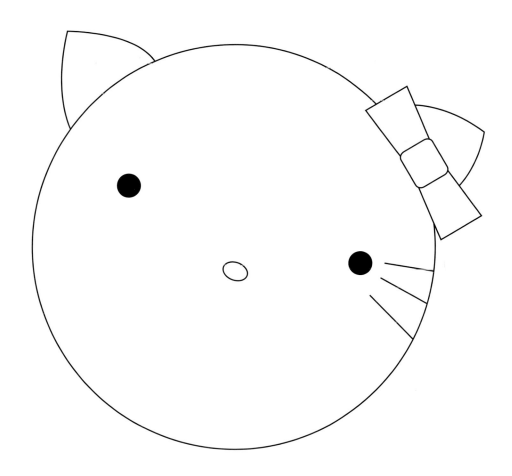

BASEBALL CAP CROWN PATTERN
(USE AT 100%)
Project instructions can
be found on page 102.

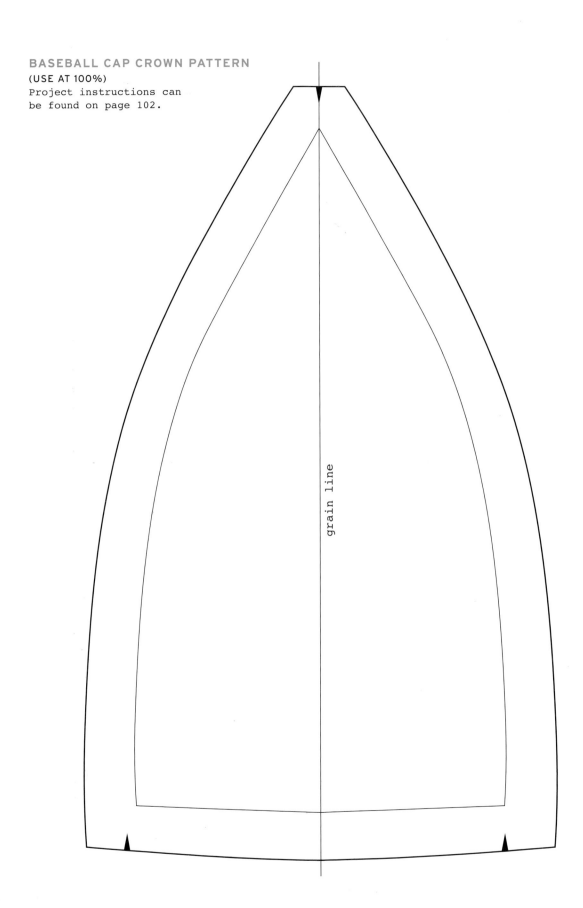

grain line

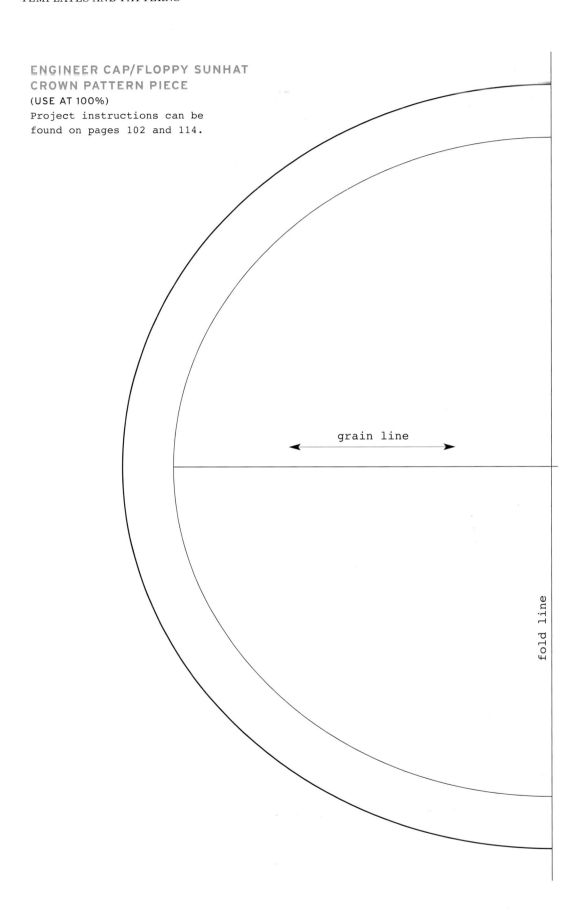

ENGINEER CAP/FLOPPY SUNHAT
CROWN PATTERN PIECE
(USE AT 100%)
Project instructions can be
found on pages 102 and 114.

grain line

fold line

CLASSIC CLOCHE PATTERN
(ENLARGE 20%)
Project instructions can
be found on page 34.

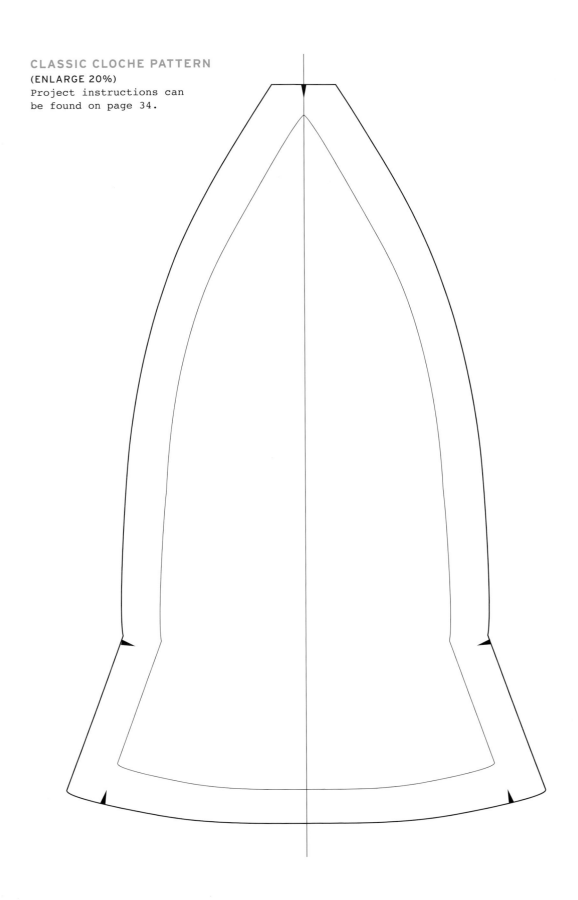

BASEBALL CAP BILL PATTERN TEMPLATE
(ENLARGE 20%)
Project instructions can be found on page 96.

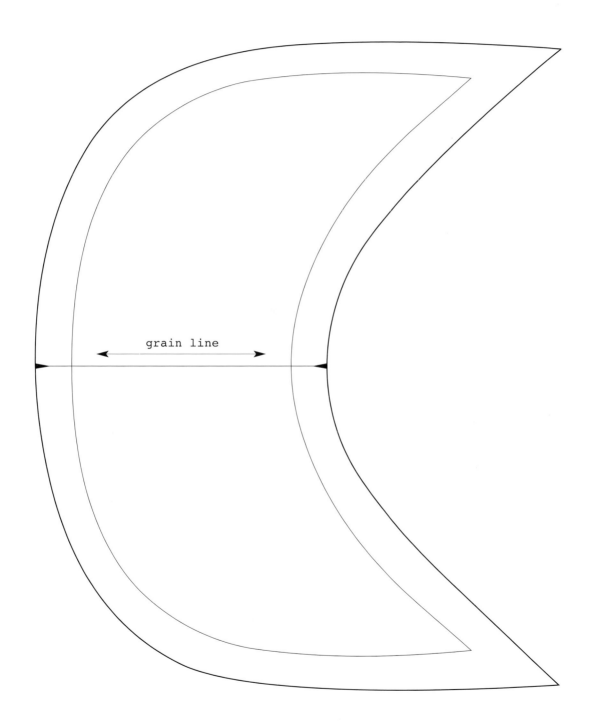

grain line

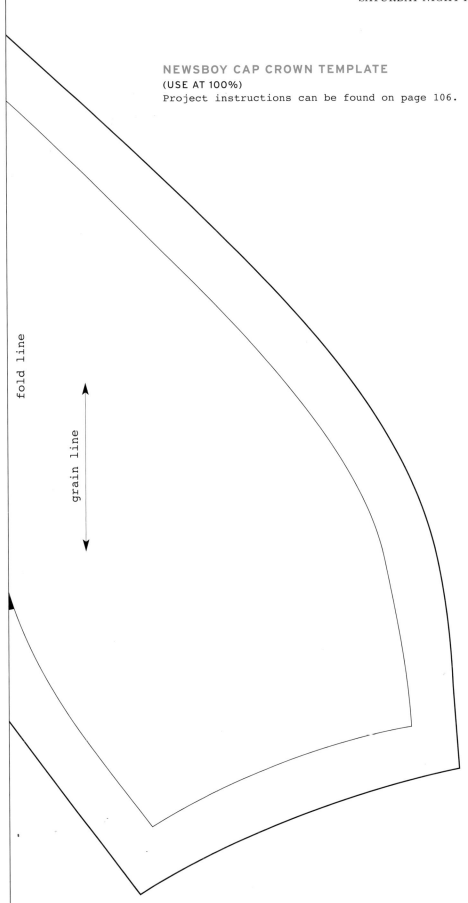

NEWSBOY CAP CROWN TEMPLATE
(USE AT 100%)
Project instructions can be found on page 106.

fold line

grain line

ENGINEER AND NEWSBOY BILL TEMPLATE
(ENLARGE 20%)
Project instructions can be found on pages 102 and 106.

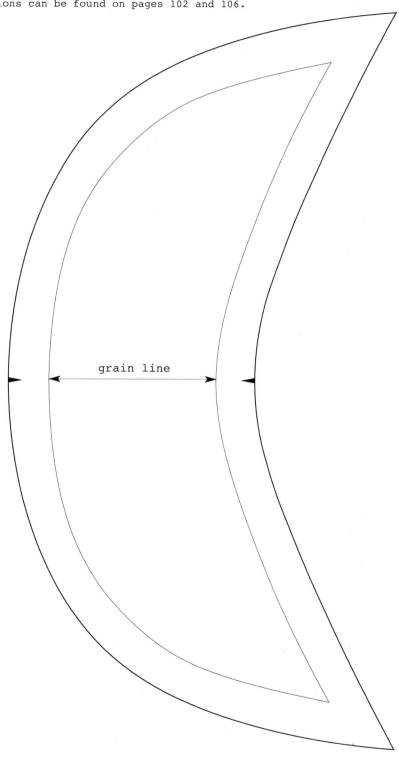

grain line

INDEX